STELIOS RIGLIS

CRETAN HEALTHY DIET

Truths and secrets

KERKYRA
publications

TABLE OF CONTENTS

ISBN: 960-8386-27-6

© KERKYRA Publications
1st English edition, August 2005

Editing: Athanasia Ziotou
Publishing coordination: Efi Andrikopoulou
Production: KERKYRA Publications
Production Manager: George Maniatogiannis
Cover design: Lefteris Malagaris
Design - Layout: MULTI PROGRESS
Slides: John Milonakis, Fanis Manousakis, Manolis Kiriakakis
English translation: Chrissoula Jemanakis
English editing: Kaliope Gourntis

Central sales outlet  **KERKYRA** publications **bookstore OIKONOMIKH**

6-8 Vlahava St. Athens GR- 105 51, Tel.: 210 - 3314.714, fax: 210-3252.283
www.oikonomiki.gr, sales@oikonomiki.gr
www.bookstore-oikonomiki.gr, bookstore@oikonomiki.gr

Introduction

The book "Cretan Healthy Diet – Truths and Secrets" constitutes a guide for supreme quality living. It is an effort to introduce the reader to Cretan cuisine and its secrets. Secrets that promise health and longevity "hidden" for thousands of years behind the shining golden olive oil, the ruby red wine, the deep golden yellow honey, the bright green vegetables, the colourful fruits and aromatic herbs.

These secrets underlie the way in which we acquire the natural products from Cretan earth, the way in which these processed products reach our table.

The primary production depends on the local community, the soil and climatic conditions, as well as the cultivation methods. It is tightly bound with tradition and the natural production of agricultural products which respects human consumers.

Cretan products are pure, of high quality and delicious. The dietary habits of Cretans that are deeply rooted in their civilisation undoubtedly provide the standards for a healthy diet. The harmonious balance between man, food and earth ought to be based upon our cultural inheritance. The adoption of this idea will contribute to the new organisation of the food management system.

It has been proven that the optimal health and longevity of Cretans is due to their traditional Cretan diet. This diet is frugal and draws its daily energy mainly from extra virgin olive oil. Over the last decades, the simple traditional Cretan diet has been altered primarily by younger generations. The Cretan diet has witnessed changes due to modern lifestyle, haste, fast foods, as well as the imported subculture that strives to corrode and level everything.

Nonetheless, not everything is the same. There are differences and the Cretan diet offers multiple comparative advantages.

This book represents an effort to record these advantages in the form of a comprehensive memory from which the younger generations can retrieve this traditional, healthy diet from the past and adapt it to modern life demands. We endeavour to document this treasure from which we derive the most precious human value, namely our health.

ACKNOWLEDGEMENTS

The entire endeavour could not have been achieved without the recipes entrusted to us by Cretan housewives. We would like to express our sincere appreciation to Maria Harhalakis, farmer, Fotini Harhalakis - Riglis, agricultural engineer, Efi Zeibekakis, professor of English Language and Literature. The recipe book of the dear departed Katerina Riglis also constituted an invaluable source for the compilation of the present book.

The photographs in the present publication are by John Milonakis, photographer, and from the archive of George Sergakis of Multi Progress. We would like to express our sincere appreciation to both.

We would also like to take the opportunity to thank the owners of the following restaurants for preparing the Cretan specialties presented in the present book for the relevant photo session: 'Kàvoura', 'Konàki', 'Neràida', 'Vàmos SA', as well as the coffee shop of Argiro Daskalakis.

FOREWORD

*Let your food be your medicine
and let medicine be your food*
Hippocrates

The book titled "Cretan Healthy Diet – Truths and Secrets" strives to highlight through its pages the widely known Cretan Diet, as it is shaped and dictated by the Cretan lifestyle, the Cretan customs and tradition and the Cretan civilization.

It demonstrates the characteristics of this supreme-quality diet made up of healthy and natural products produced by the Cretan Earth, such as olive oil, wine, vegetable and fruits, as well as aromatic herbs.

It initiates the reader into the wonderful world of Cretan tastes, namely the "pleasant", as well as the natural authentic ingredients making up these tastes and ensuring optimal health and longevity, namely the "useful".

In our age of stress and a hectic pace of life, our diet has succumbed to the dictations of the tasteless and unhealthy fast food. Now, more than ever, it is imperative that the Cretan diet, resembling a mythical Siren calling out from the coasts of our island, invites everyone to initiate into a lifestyle of insurmountable quality through the aromas, the colours and the exquisite tastes of Cretan specialties.

This book brings forth the local dietary tradition with its authentic flavours and the use of excellent local products, which finally lead to the love and enjoyment of life itself.

THE PREFECT OF HANIA
GEORGE KATSANEVAKIS

The Myth of Europa

Once upon a time, in the very old days, when great Zeus was the father of gods and men, Agenor was king of the East. Agenor had three sons and a daughter, Europa. She was so beautiful that even goddess Aphrodite was jealous of her.

The Great Zeus, overcome by Europa's beauty and grace decided to abduct her to the West. He ordered god Oneiron (Dream) to appear in Europa's dream one night to find out whether she would be willing to forsake her father's palace. In this dream two women, East and West, were arguing over Europa. If the arguments of East prevailed, Europa would stay in Asia, in the kingdom of her parents. Otherwise, Europa would have to follow West to a place beyond the deep blue sea, where each night the sun sets in all its glory. Assisted by Zeus, the arguments of West prevailed over those of the other contestant. Shattered by the knowledge of Europa's imminent departure, East, bid farewell to the noble princess, whose beauty was a jewel for the entire continent of Asia.

Disturbed by the dream, Europa woke up frightened. She would not leave her birthplace and parents she loved so much for anything in the world. However, the will of Zeus could hardly be contested by any human means. He crafted a plan to abduct the fair princess of Phoenicia.

It was a sunny day when Europa and her companions, all daughters of nobility, went off gathering flowers by the sea enjoying the beautiful landscape. Suddenly, a magnificent white bull appeared before the group. The bull lay down in front of Europa. Curious as she was, she approached the pretty creature. She climbed upon his back and, instantly, the bull charged off, plunging into the sea carrying the object of his affection over the waves to Crete.

Since then, the area extending from Crete over to mainland Greece and to the shores of the continent that is drenched by the waters of the great ocean in the west was named Europe, after the beautiful princess of Phoenicia, Europa.

The bull was nobody else but Zeus, the king of Gods, transformed into a bull. From the union of Zeus and Europa Minos was born, the renowned king of Crete. In this sense, Europa became the fountainhead of one of the world's oldest civilizations in the Mediterranean basin, the Minoan Civilization, and gave her name to an entire continent and civilization, the European civilisation, that was destined to change the world.

Nutrition: A Fundamental Element of Culture

An essential element of the Minoan civilization was the nutritional habits of the people and the particular way they consumed the products they produced in that remote era.

Nutritional habits are part and parcel of culture and tradition.

Not only did philosophy, letters and music take root on Crete, but so did sound and healthy nutrition.

Gastronomy is basically culturally determined, fashioned with the threads of memory, morals and customs, history, attitudes to life and personal relations.

Today, with technology working miracles, we can apply chemical processes to analyse organic residues in the soil, clay and bones to learn more not only about the dietary habits of our ancestors, but also about their gender, age, physical characteristics and establish causes of death by analysing their DNA sequence.

Chemical analyses of food residues found in the soil and ancient clay vessels show that the inhabitants of the island for thousands of years, since Cretans lived in caves, consumed large quantities of olive oil, vegetables, honey, wine, fish, pulses and cereals.

This is also true of the Minoan period.

Professor P. Warren of Bristol University claims that the structure of the Cretan diet has remained essentially the same since the Copper Age, i.e. for the last 5000 years. During the course of history other foodstuffs were introduced into the Cretan diet: rice, tomatoes, potatoes, fruits, and the avocado.

Perhaps it would be interesting at this point to make a reference to some notes taken by people who visited Crete in the past. These people currently referred to as "travellers" put their thoughts and impressions of the island and its inhabitants on paper, in diaries. These diaries constitute invaluable sources of information for scientists who study history, folklore and the nutritional habits of Cretans.

The Travellers

F.W. Sieber was a physician and a fervent amateur botanist. He was of Austrian origin but born in Prague. In his diaries there are references to the Akrotìri of Hania and to the monks of the St. Trinity (Agia Triàda) Monastery there. He notes that the monks made bread from wheat, barley and secale creticum (rye), which had a distinctive but pleasant taste, and that he was treated to the best Malvasia wine he had ever tasted. This wine of the Archipelago sparkled like gold, he continued, evoking the nectar of the gods born on this island. The Malvasia wine was produced only in Crete and exported mainly to Germany, England and France. As the wine turned sour along its export routes, the people of Rethymnon would boil it in large cauldrons before it was taken abroad. Wine exports to Italy were mainly through the ports of Heraklion and Hania, the two largest cities of Crete, but the local exporters seldom boiled the wine before shipment.

In 1792, the French revolutionary government organised a trade expedition in the territories of the Ottoman Empire. The aim was to collect as much information as possible about people, trade prospects and culture.

In his two-volume chronicle, a large part of which is dedicated to Crete, **Guillaume Antoine Olivier** (1756-1814) mentions the following about the nutritional habits of Cretans:

Although the leaves of the bean plant are consumed nowhere on the island today, yet in the older days people used to cook or fry them in olive oil. The leaves of the chickpea plant were either cooked or used for salad. This kind of food is unknown today, but the chickpeas themselves are cooked in various ways; they are even consumed raw or just before they dry up. People living in the countryside consume even today the courgette flowers, fried or stuffed with rice and/or ground coarse wheat. The vine leaves were cooked and also preserved in vinegar. Today they are stuffed. In some areas of the island people consume the young shoots and leaves of the vine, along with other greens lending them a sourish taste. People also used to cook radish leaves. Today they are only consumed raw. The mustard leaves and shoots, as well as those of a large number of the cruciferae family, are consumed (cooked or fried) even today. The leaves and tender shoots of the wild asparagus, the black nightshade, the mallow, the poppy flower ('koutsounàda'), the wild amaranth, the bluebell, the fennel (raw or preserved in vinegar), the tomatoes, the leaves and buds of caper (without its thorns) are preserved in vinegar, and many more … are part of the Cretan diet even today.

The French traveller adds that the Cretans of that period consumed among others the leaves and tender shoots of prickly bushes, the ears of corns, the roots of parsley.

Hourmouzis the Byzantine (1842) notes that Cretans consume meat often, but also makes specific mention to cultivated and wild greens, which he believes have positive health benefits for Cretans, as is the case with barley bread. He also notes that Cretans use olive oil "in excess".

However, the person who managed to present in a most vivid manner the dietary habits of Cretans was the English **R. Pashley** (1837). He came to the island during the period of the Greek Revolution (1821) and witnessed the harsh living conditions of the inhabitants.

His description of a meal offered to some guests in the province of Apokòronas is quite revealing: "…since the eggs were a rare commodity it took some time to find a few for the guests. The guests' meal also included olives and barley bread. The host and his wife limited themselves to boiled wild greens in olive oil, which seems to be the staple part of the Cretans' diet". The same traveller had eggs and salad from wild asparagus for dinner at Kìssamos, while at Sèlino he found out that boiled greens, sprinkled with olive oil, and barley bread constitute the staple diet of Cretans.

Raulin (1869), another traveller, had his first okra and meat dish at the village of Kritsà, province of Meràbelo, and relished it.

In 1896 the epidemiologist Henri Blackburn wrote the following:

"Allow me to describe the average inhabitant on the island of Crete. He is either a stockbreeder or a farmer. He goes to work on foot at the crack of dawn, ever so sweet in Crete, and toils in the quiet of his land disturbed only by the humming of cicadas. After a good half-day's work, he seeks refuge in the village cafe (kafenìo) where he joins close friends (koumbàroi*) in conversation, drinks lemonade and smokes a cigarette he rolls himself. After lunch he takes a siesta for a couple of hours, to wake up invigorated for the latter part of the day's work.

His meals at home consist of eggplants, mushrooms, crunchy vegetables and bread dipped in olive oil. He has lamb or chicken once a week and fish twice a week. Among other hot dishes in his diet are the legumes cooked either with meat or as a stand-alone meal with a little condiment. His main course is normally accompanied with salad, olives, syrupy pastries, and dried or fresh fruit. The local wine comes to wrap up this diverse and palatable diet. Saturday nights are an occasion for a more festive dinner in the company of friends and relatives.

---

*The word koumbàroi /koubàros/ is used in Greek to literally refer to the godfather or the best man. However, it also carries the connotation of 'friend'.

The merry-making winds up to dancing in the moonlight after midnight hours. On Sunday our average Cretan goes to church with his wife and children. Impressed by the pulpit speech, he goes back home early in the afternoon to enjoy the rest of the day in the company of his family and the scent of the richly, seasoned with herbs meat on charcoal. In this harmonious, but wild landscape, the Cretan feels safe.
He wallows in the natural and repetitive cycles that form the basis of his culture: work and rest, isolation and companionship, austerity and gaiety, routine and feasting. In his old age he basks in the golden light of the sun in recline. He is handsome, rough, endearing and virile. He is least likely to suffer from a coronary hear disease; his mortality rate is low and ranks high in longevity in relation to other westerners."

This information reveals the extent to which Cretans depend on nature in terms of food and well-being.

The Research on the Ideal Diet

The Cretan diet has attracted international interest.

In its search for the ideal diet, one that would promote health and prevent the onset of various diseases, the international research community established, in the wake also of the Seven Countries Study launched by physician Ancel Keys, that the habitual diet of Cretans brings together all those characteristics that render it not only suitable, but also ideal for maintaining excellent health.

The Seven Countries Study started in the 1950's in the form of surveys in population groups of 100,000 individuals between the ages of 40 and 59, pooled from 16 areas of the seven countries: 2 study groups from Greece, 3 from Italy, 5 from the former Yugoslavia, 2 from Japan, 2 from Finland, 1 from the Netherlands and 1 from the USA.

One of the two Greek study groups was pooled from the island of Crete and the other from the island of Corfu. The selection of these two Greek regions was based on the fact that these areas manifested significant differences in terms of overall development.

In the 1960's, the Cretans still maintained their traditional Greek dietary habits, uninfluenced by western life styles.

The above-mentioned study lasted for a number of years and drew comparative conclusions about the populations' longevity (mortality rates), heart diseases, cancer and overall mortality.

The results were published 10 and 15 years later. On the basis of those results, the Cretans manifested the lowest morbidity rates in terms of cardiovascular diseases, cancer and overall mortality.

At follow-up 15 years later, the study revealed that 38 members of the Crete group died from coronary heart diseases (CHD) compared with 202 from the Corfu group, 242 from Former Yugoslavia, 462 from Italy and 773 from the USA. During the same period, mortality from cancer was 317 for Crete, 338 for Corfu, 394 for former Yugoslavia, 662 for Italy and 384 for the USA. Total death rates amounted to 855 for Crete, 1317 for Corfu, 1712 for former Yugoslavia, 1874 for Italy and 1575 for the USA.

The second lowest death rate from cardiovascular diseases was 136 for Japan, compared with 38 for Crete. However, the Japanese group manifested higher mortality from cancer (623 subjects), which matched that of the Italian group.

The statistical results from the Seven Countries Study do not deviate significantly from those of the World Health Organization, as seen in the following Tables.

Table 1: Death rates recorded in cohort groups in a period of 15 years after the commencement of the Seven Countries Study.

Per 100,000 subjects	CORONARY HEART DISEASE	CANCER	OVERALL MORTALITY
Finnland	972	613	2169
USA	773	384	1575
Zutphen (the Netherlands)	636	781	1825
Italy	462	622	1874
Former Yugoslavia	242	394	1712
Corfu (Greece)	202	338	1317
Japan	136	623	1766
Crete (Greece)	38	317	855

Adjusted by:

A. Keys et al., 1986.

Table 2: Mortality rates from coronary heart disease and overall mortality per 100,000 subjects.

	Seven Countries Study (10 years)		(1987) World Health Organization	
	Coronary Heart Disease	Overall MORTALITY	Coronary Heart Disease	Overall MORTALITY
Finland	466	1390	386	1210
USA	424	961	263	1061
The Netherlands	317	1134	224	1016
Italy	200	1092	148	1066
Former Yugoslavia	145	1021	137	1302
Corfu (Greece)	149	847	123	932
Japan	61	1200	53	837
Crete (Greece)	9	627	7	564

Table 2 was compiled on the basis of 10-year results from the Seven Countries Study and statistical information from WHO (1987).

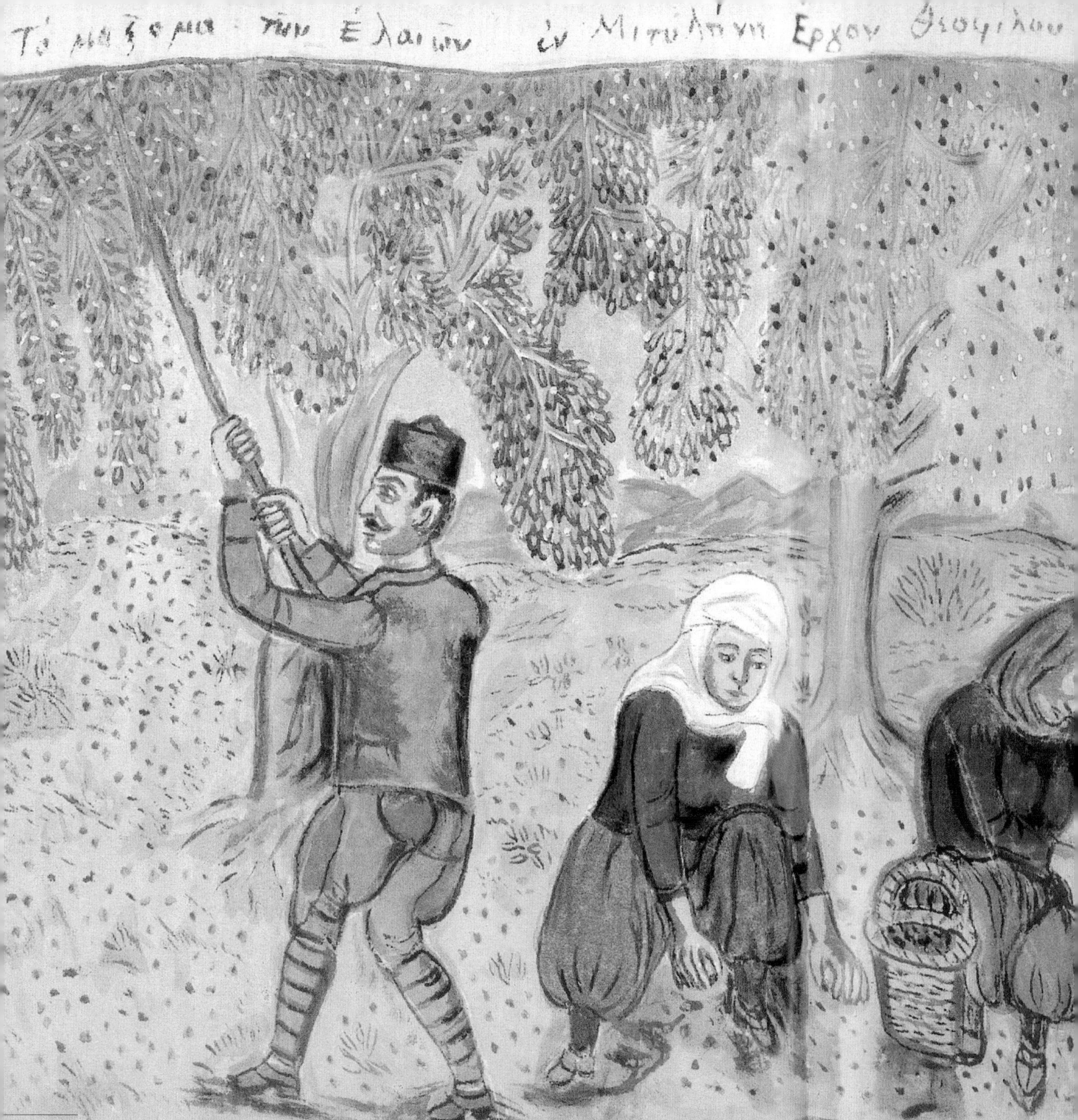
Τό μαζεμα τῶν Ἐλαιῶν ἐν Μιτυλήνη Ἔργον Θεοφίλου

The Cretan Diet

The good health and marked longevity of Cretans, particularly of the older generation, is attributed to their traditional diet. Unfortunately, the younger generation has succumbed to foreign dietary styles (fast food) that undermine their health.

The Cretan diet consists mainly of olive oil, cereals, legumes, vegetables, fruit and small quantities of eggs, cheese, milk, meat and fish eaten with a little red wine.

Following the study of the dietary habits in Crete, researchers coined the term 'Cretan Diet', which applies to Greece as a whole in relation to the period of the study. Since then, the Cretan diet has become the standard for a healthy diet.

It involves the intake of 1900 to 2300 calories per day, mainly from vegetable sources:

vegetables, in large amounts
- fruits, daily
- legumes, greens, cereals and bread in large amounts
- plenty of virgin olive oil (rich in monounsaturated fatty acids)
- moderate consumption of wine at lunch/ dinner
- moderate consumption of milk and dairy products
- low consumption of meat (once a week) and higher consumption of fish in coastal areas.

The Pyramid of the Mediterranean Diet

Extensive, past research has contributed significantly to establishing relationships between dietary habits and health. We should mention at this point that a Body Mass Index (BMI) of 25kg/cm² (WHO 1985 and WHO 1990) or lower, is a requirement for maintaining good health in adult years.

The term Body Mass Index is the ratio of one's body weight in kilograms to the square of his/her height in centimetres. The Body Mass Index of an individual does not exceed 25kg/cm², when, for instance, a person measuring 180cm, 170cm and 160cm in height does not weigh more than 75kg, 65kg and 55kg, respectively. A BMI that gradually drops below 25kg/cm² is not associated with increased mortality rates, but could be considered an advantage, unless it falls under 20kg/cm². There is a plethora of data prescribing ideal caloric intake, but consumers are not expected to do calculations on a daily basis. As a rule of thumb, the higher the BMI in a person the more that person is in need of physical activity. Reducing caloric intake to maintain an ideal BMI is a secondary consideration. Physical activity is also required when the BMI has stabilized below 25kg/cm², such as: rigorous walking, swimming, dancing, climbing stairs or gardening for fifteen to thirty minutes each day.

The WHO adopted the research work on the Mediterranean Diet of the scientific committee who, in collaboration with the Harvard School of Public Health, compiled the Mediterranean Diet Pyramid.

The Mediterranean Diet Pyramid makes the following recommendations for our daily nutritional needs:

8 small servings* of minimally processed cereals and related products (whole grain bread, husked rice, etc.), 6 servings of vegetables and greens, 3 servings of season fruits. It also recommends virgin olive oil as the main source of fat and 4 small servings of red meat per month. In addition, according to the Mediterranean Diet Pyramid we should drink a lot of water and instead of salt use herbs (oregano, basil, thyme, etc.). Last but not least, physical exercise is a prerequisite for maintaining health.

Physical activity increases life expectancy.

In the 1960's, the Cretans walked on average 13km daily, which contrasts sharply with the fact that modern Cretans, either living in the countryside or in urban areas, walk less than two kilometres a day on average.

One (1) small serving is roughly equal to one half of a restaurant portion, which is equivalent to one of the following:

- *one slice of bread (25gr)*
- *100gr potatoes*
- *1/2 tea-cup (50-60gr) of cooked rice or pasta*
- *one tea-cup of leafy vegetables or 1/2 tea-cup of other vegetables, either cooked or raw (i.e. approx. 100gr of most vegetables)*
- *one apple (80gr), one banana (60gr), one orange (100gr), melon or watermelon (200gr), grapes (30gr)*
- *one tea-cup milk or yoghurt*
- *30gr cheese*
- *1 egg*
- *60gr cooked lean meat or fish*
- *one tea-cup (100gr) of cooked lima beans*

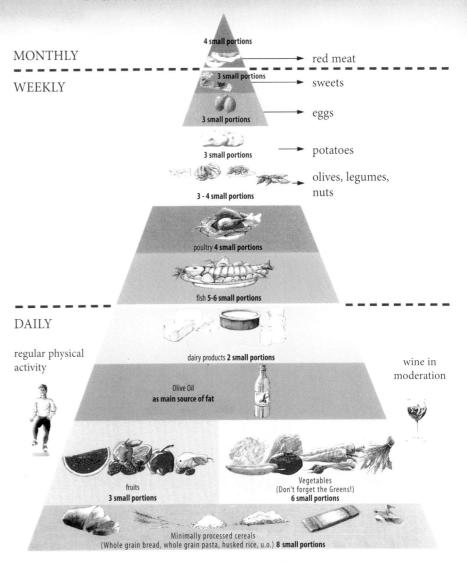

Traditional Mediterranean Diet

MONTHLY — 4 small portions → red meat

WEEKLY — 3 small portions → sweets

3 small portions → eggs

3 small portions → potatoes

3 - 4 small portions → olives, legumes, nuts

poultry 4 small portions

fish 5-6 small portions

DAILY

regular physical activity

dairy products 2 small portions

Olive Oil as main source of fat

wine in moderation

fruits 3 small portions

Vegetables (Don't forget the Greens!) 6 small portions

Minimally processed cereals (Whole grain bread, whole grain pasta, husked rice, u.o.) 8 small portions

One (1) small serving is roughly equal to one half of a restaurant portion
Also: • Drink plenty of water • Avoid salt
• Use herbs (oregano, basil, thyme, etc.) instead.

Source: Supreme Special Scientific Health Council, Ministry for Health and Social Services

PRINTED BY THE MINISTRY FOR AGRICULTURE

The Cretan Diet and Mediterranean Diets

The Mediterranean dietary habits combine, fitness, physical well-being and good health. The Cretan diet provides the inspiration for good nutrition and love for a long and healthy life. We have already mentioned that Crete, with its ancient Greek and Minoan civilizations, became the fountainhead of the European civilization. To this we should add that the habitual diet of the Cretans provided the standards for healthy nutrition, i.e. became the core of the Mediterranean diet.

In November 2002, the prefecture of Hania organized an international conference - "Mediterranean: Common points and differences in the context of a rich cultural tradition" - in the town of Hania where specialists from Italy, France, Spain and Malta had been invited to present their papers. In the section devoted to the Mediterranean diet, the experts concluded that the term Mediterranean Diet should be used to mean Mediterranean Diets. Indeed, there is neither a unique diet, nor a standard nutrition for all. Each person has his/her own nutritional requirements, which are determined by his/her age, weight, blood results, activities, type of exercise, occupation, fitness level, heredity and other factors, i.e. life-style, the local climate, local products and religious prescriptions.

Consequently, there are numerous Mediterranean Diets that fit into the Mediterranean Diet Pyramid.

However, the Cretan dietary tradition, which makes "excessive" use of olive oil, legumes and fruit, forms the basis of all Mediterranean diets. More than 33% of all energy-intake through the Cretan Diet comes exclusively from virgin olive oil.

During the last few years, it has become common knowledge that various aspects of the Mediterranean Diet, in particular olive oil combined with vegetables and legumes, can offer significant protection against a wide range of chronic diseases.

We should note at this point that the traditional products of Crete, and Greece in general, meet the highest standards for foodstuffs, as well as the protected designation of origin (PDO) and are labelled accordingly. Moreover, they are healthy and reliable. To this effect they are in high demand in European and American markets.

The local governments of the country should encourage discussions and planning that would set local production on a new footing and help consumers make informed choices. Currently, the people are aware of the following classification of products:

a. Genetically modified: these products are intended for mass consumption targeting low-income groups.

b. Biological or organic: products certified for their health benefits and nutritional value, but targeting high income consumers.

c. Traditional: products distinguished for their excellent taste and health benefits. These products are consumed mostly by people that are producers themselves as well as by informed consumers. Crete is synonymous with traditional farming and healthy dietary habits.

The Cretan Diet and the Christian Orthodox Tradition

What is particular about the Cretan Diet is the fact that it is directly linked to the Christian Orthodox tradition. In other words, the particular diet follows the cycles of fasting and religious holidays as laid down in the Calendar of the Orthodox Church.

Let us see what is the case with pork at Christmas in the context of the Orthodox tradition. Traditionally, meat eating at Christmas came after a long period of fasting (40 days), during which meat was banned from the dinner tables of Cretans. Each family in the countryside raised its own pig that was slaughtered on Christmas Eve. Pork is rich in proteins and the meat from an average size animal sufficed to cover the particular nutritional requirements of the families for the entire holiday period. These fatty traditional pork delicacies as *omathiés*, sausages, *apàkia*, have not managed to spoil the good reputation of the Cretan Diet.

The *omathiés* delicacies (or *ematiés* of the Byzantines) were produced from a pig's long intestine, entrails and blood. The entrails were boiled and stuffed in the animal's intestine. The Church had banned the use of blood in meals, but this did not discourage the Byzantines from keeping in line with tradition. Leo VI, the wise emperor of the Byzantine Empire, had decreed that all those who consumed or sold food made from blood would be subjected to punishment involving the cutting off of their hair, public ridicule, flogging and confiscation of their property. Following numerous admonitions and decrees, the use of blood in meals gradually waned in Constantinople. However, dietary habits with deep roots in history were not to die out completely. They survived in the remotest regions of the empire and passed from one generation to another. Currently, blood recipes are encountered in the Greek speaking regions of lower Italy (Calabria).

Meat and meat products have not been central to the Cretan diet. This role had been preserved for bread, the *Christòpsomo* (Christ's bread). Cretans have always had a soft spot for ceremonial breads. The bread items dedicated to newborn Christ were masterpieces of bakery and art. There was much love that went into the process of kneading – a process carried out in the context of tradition and faith that resulted in richly decorated loaves of bread. The decorative elements on a *Christòpsomo* were fashioned in dough to resemble crosses, ploughs, animal yokes, the Cretan lyre and bells for sheep and goats.

In some regions in south-central Crete, bread decorations included an imitation of a small tree laden with fruit – all made of dough.

This custom is a direct reference to the worship of trees in Crete in prehistoric times. This custom has survived to this day.

Although pork cooked with wild greens, celery and *skioufihtà* pasta, etc. was the main dish for Cretans from the day after Christmas to New Year's Day, other dishes were also served during this holiday period. Legumes, greens and pasta had been on the daily dietary agenda of Cretans for years.

With the exception of Christmas Day, Cretans had no customary dish for New Year's Day. Holiday dietary customs varied, but one could always find *pichtì*, a kind of meat jelly, on most dinner tables.

The Cretan households returned to normal routines and diet the day after New Year's Day. Preserved pork leftovers, sausages and *sìglina*, provided an ample source of calories during the cold winter nights.

Religious feasts in the month of January were unique occasions associated with meat consumption only in areas where churches dedicated to Epiphany, Saint (Agios) Antonios, Saint Athanàsios, and the Three Hierarchs existed. In other respects, meat was consumed mainly on Sundays.

On Carnival Sunday (Apokreò), or the day before, all households cooked meat from kids or from larger animals (pigs, calves), or poultry. However, those who observed religious ordinances abstained from eating meat during that period. A few days before Apokreò Cretan housewives were busy preparing food that was allowed during the days of fasting.

The Lent was a period of strict fasting and abstinence. Olive oil was allowed in most days of the week except Wednesdays and Fridays. During Lent, the Cretans subsisted only on bread, snails and/or fish. The occasional chance guests were treated to dried fruit, nuts and oil biscuits. The same frugal diet was also served on special occasions as well.

The Cretans were very frugal during the period of Lent, observing a strict nutritional regimen. Lunch consisted of greens or legumes cooked in very imaginative ways, while dinner was light, consisting mainly of pasta. Such preparations as *magìri, hìlos, hilopìtes, triftoùdia* and lasagne were the main Cretan pasta or pasta-like dishes on Sundays and leisure days during the same holiday period.

The 25th of March is a very important holiday for the Greek Orthodox Church. It has been a national holiday for the Greeks since the mid-19th century, when in 1821 the Greeks revolted against the Turks to win their independence. The same holds true for the Cretans who observed the celebrations even when they were under Turkish rule. On that day, the Cretans living in urban centres and coastal areas preferred fish, provided that the weather allowed fish markets to stock up. They had devised numerous ways of cooking codfish, referred to as *ftohoyiànnis* (ftochòs=poor, Yiànnis=John).

The Holy Passion during the Holy Week was a heart-felt experience that brought Cretans closer to understanding the suffering of Jesus. It was a time for contemplation and reflection. During that period, the Cretans observed strict fasting. The housewives would spend little time in the kitchen and food was restricted to raw greens, bread and olives. For example, on Holy Friday Cretans would abstain from almost all kinds of food; they would not even sit at the dinner table.

On Holy Saturday they prepared the Easter lamb, the *kalitsoùnia* and other pastries for the great feast, while the Easter eggs had been dyed in Madder, *rizàri* in Greek, a plant resourced locally, since Holy Thursday.

After seven weeks on a regimen of greens and

vegetables, the Easter lamb was relished to the bone.

Following the vigil of the resurrection on Holy Saturday, the Cretans would return from church in the early Sunday morning hours to sit at a sumptuous dinner table. In those early Easter Day hours the first dish was *magirìtsa*, a preparation common all over Greece. However, *magirìtsa* was foreign to the popular Cretan cuisine. It was first mentioned as an Easter meal favoured by the urban families of the island in the 19th century. This shows that Easter meals were not the same all over the island: they ranged from *magirìtsa, to gardoùmia or kokorétsi,* chicken soup or roast meat in home ovens fired in the afternoon of the same day. The lamb had been set aside for the following day, Easter Sunday. On many mountainous regions the lamb was roasted on the spit, which is a national custom. Alternatively, the lamb was cooked in home ovens. In any case, the meals on this great feast day included (and still does) ofto meat. Lets examine this particular way of meat cooking. Basically, *oftò* means cooked on charcoal. This refers to the ancient Greek *optò* (currently *oftò*) method of devotional offering, which involved the digging of a small trench on the ground, the lining of its perimeter with stones as support for the offering on the spit and the cooking of the meat in the fire kindled in the middle of the trench. Also, the use of spits is an ancient custom. The use of spits is a direct reference to spears used by the ancient Greek warriors to skewer their meat and cook it over open-air fires. However, the shepherds on Mt. Psilorìtis on Crete are rather impatient with the entire process of cooking the *oftò*. They will not wait for the charcoals to burn to ashes and then cook the meat, as is the custom on mainland Greece. They are gluttonous and cannot wait until the meat is done. They consume it rather raw or half done. This attitude to cooking *oftò* is rooted in history, in the period of Turkish occupation. In those days, starting a fire to cook the meat was risky, since the billowing smoke would reveal the position of the Cretan rebels of that time (*haìnides*) to the Turks. Notwithstanding the risks, the rebels skewered their meat on spits, cooked it fast on live fire and consumed it just as fast…

The shepherds on the Madàres range would follow a different method in preparing oftς meat. They would dig a somewhat deeper hole in the ground, where they started a fire and would wait until the charcoals were totally burnt out. The people of the remote Sfakià area did not cook their meat on live fire or on charcoal in trenches. They were not afraid of the Turks, as the latter were daunted by the ragged terrain in the area (high mountains and deep gorges).

The most common Easter meal in the Cretan countryside is not the *oftò*, but lamb stew,

while meat pies are served on Easter Sunday in Hania. The meat pies are very palatable as they are made from local meat and dairy products. On the Easter feast table one can also see bread made especially for the occasion, i.e. *Labrokouloùra*, a round Easter bread, *kalitsoùnia* (usually salty) or *lihnaràkia* (usually sweet).

The week following Easter, the Bright Week (Diakainìsimos), constituted a fast free period, an occasion for meat consumption. The globular thistle-like heads of the artichoke plant are mature this time of year, and Cretans cook them in various ways.

There was a special diet set for the Bright Week, particularly on the Zoodòchos Pigi (Life-giving source) feast day, with celebrations taking place in remote chapels near springs. The feasts were significant occasions for meat eating (*oftò*). Meat was consumed also on Thomas Sunday. After that day the Cretans' diet changed, as the first signs of spring began making their presence felt on land and in the air. It is the time of year that the vines bear fresh and tender leaves, which are collected by Cretans to prepare the traditional *Dolmadàkia* dish. In the past, the vine leaves were stuffed with ground wheat, while in modern days they are stuffed with rice. Stuffed vine leaves are a spring delicacy. The meat is cooked with various greens, e.g. tender vine sprigs, fresh potatoes, fennel, dill, etc. In summer, with its plethora of religious feasts, Cretans have more opportunities for meat eating. Meat was usually braised in tomato sauce, broiled or cooked *oftò*. On such saints' feast days as Agia Marina, Agia Paraskevi and Agios Panteleimonas, the scent from meat roasting in neighbourhood bakeries tantalized the senses. On August 1st begins a fasting period of fifteen days until the Assumption of Virgin Mary. The diet of the Cretans during that period is quite frugal: rice, *hòndros*, a lot of vegetables, as well as fish and snails. The Assumption of Virgin Mary, celebrated on August 15, is a major holiday in all parts of Greece. *Oftò*, broiled meat or meat braised with tomato sauce, is present on all dinner tables, with meat pies supplementing the meals on the western part of the island.

The feast of Agios Dimitrios is in autumn, during which pork with celery is cooked.

The period of 40 days of fasting before Christmas is not considered as significant as Lent. It is interspersed with major feasts, e.g. Agios Nikolaos, Agios Eleftherios, etc. celebrated during this period. The Church, but also weather permitting, allows the consumption of fish or salt cod.

The Orthodox Church has established the following strict fasting periods, and rightly so since fasting is good for one's health:

Christmas fasting

It spans from 15 November to 24 December during which meat, dairy products and fish are not allowed. The same is true for olive oil and wine on Wednesdays and Fridays during the same period. Fish is allowed on Saturdays and Sundays from 21 November (fore feast of the Presentation of Virgin Mary) until 12 December (Saint Spirìdon).

Great 40 day fasting (Lent-Tessarakostì)

It is a 40-day period starting from the end of February (Clean Monday-Katharà Deftèra) to Holy Saturday, during which Cretans abstain from eating meat, dairy products, fish, oil and wine. Oil and wine are allowed on Saturdays and Sundays (except Holy Saturday). Fish is allowed on March 25 (Annunciation of Virgin Mary).

Holy Apostles fasting

It is the period from Monday following All Saints (Sunday, June 6) to the eve of the Apostles Peter and Paul (June 28). Also, olive oil and wine are not allowed on Wednesdays and Thursdays during the same period. Fish is allowed on Saturdays and Sundays

Virgin Mary Fasting

The period from August 1st to August 14th Cretans abstain from meat, dairy products, fish, olive oil and wine. The latter two are allowed only on Saturdays and Sundays of the same period. Also, fish is allowed on 6 August, the feast of the Holy Transfiguration.

Finally, Cretans abstain from meat, dairy products, fish, olive oil and wine every Wednesday and Friday throughout the year, including the following days:

- *September 14: Exaltation of the Holy Cross*
- *December 24: Christmas Eve*
- *January 5: Eve of the Epiphany*
- *August 29: Beheading of John the Baptist*

Should the above dates fall on a Saturday or Sunday, then olive oil and wine are allowed.

The week after Easter, the Bright Week, as well as the week after the Pentecost-Trinity (Sunday) to All Saints (Sunday) are fast free.

The Cretan Diet and the Four Seasons of the Year

Some of the elements constituting the Cretan diet render it unique. The Cretan diet is simple and sufficient, practical and expedient, suitable both for the poor and the rich. It is also space independent, with product requirements that can fit into a little pouch or take up a large wood table.

The Cretan diet is for times of peace and times of war; it is for all year round.

• The Winter diet includes a lot of legumes, wild greens, pork, soups, salt cod, snails, pasta.

• The Spring diet includes less legumes, while fresh broad beans, artichokes, fish, lamb and goat are added.

• The Summer diet is rich in vegetables, fruits and salads. *Mizithra* cheese replaces other types of cheese, marries well with vegetables and is excellent for breakfast. *Hòndros* is one of the favourite dairy preparations of the summer season. It is consumed fresh or is air-dried for later use.

• The Autumn diet constitutes the continuation of the summer diet until the early winter produce (vegetables, cauliflower, leeks, etc.)

Demand for legumes, radishes, salads, cauliflower and wild greens (raw or boiled) peaked in the month of January. On the eve of the Epiphany (January 5) the Cretans all over the island cooked a special dish referred to as photopàpouda or *psarokòliva* or *palikària*. The latter term is a direct reference to the ancient Greek *polispòria*, a kind of thick vegetable soup made from boiled legumes, such as broad beans, chickpeas, beans, lentils, etc. The soup was oil-free (for fasting) but sprinkled with chopped dill and onions. This meal was shared with the family livestock.

Cretans living near coastal areas consumed a lot of fish, provided the weather allowed a good catch.

There were ample supplies of salt cod and sardines but their use was rather restricted in the old days.

Nonetheless, the coastal populations, in contrast to those living in remote mountainous villages where fish hardly ever made it fresh, rarely preferred this kind of fish.

The February diet did not deviate significantly from that of January. During the second month of the year people consumed a lot of legumes and vegetables, often accompanied by dairy products and milk. Pasta in milk and *Hòndros* were also consumed. During this month, homesteads were well stocked with fresh milk they produced themselves. In February the Cretans celebrate the Apokreò Day, which is associated with unique culinary preparations. February and March are the months that Cretans consume a lot of greens. The February rains cause a riot in vegetation all over the island. The local flora comprises scores of edible greens that the Cretan imagination has harnessed to an equal number of preparations: boiled, sautéed, in tomato paste, mixed with meat, snails, fish, etc.

In spring, the Cretan diet involves a lot of greens and fish; the consumption of legumes wanes and meals are much lighter, enriched with fresh broad beans and peas.

The first of May was celebrated in a unique way. In the morning, families would have *sarantadèndri* or *sarantavòtano* for breakfast: a dessert made from forty herbs, hence its prefix *'sarànta'* meaning forty in Greek. According to popular beliefs, the application of number forty in daily routines could ward off spells since the month of May was associated with magic. The Cretans would toss the forty herbs in a clay bowl, add honey and milk and place the bowl on the roof of their house, outside the cats' reach, so that the light of the stars would shine on them for a few nights. The use of honey and milk was symbolic, as both ingredients were thought to incorporate the magic of number forty: according to popular belief bees draw nectar from 40 flowers. In the same vein of magic-religious thought, goats and sheep graze on forty plants.

The summer offers a richer variety of products to the Cretan household. Vegetables that barely need cultivation, e.g. the black nightshade, the wild amaranth, the purslane (antràkla) can be picked from roadsides and trenches. Cretans are mainly vegetarian and can hardly do without herbs and vegetables even when they are out of season. The purslane is consumed raw, mixed with other greens to make salads, but also cooked. It has found a warm spot in the heart of the Cretans. The black nightshade and the wild amaranth are cooked with potatoes, but also used in herb pies around the island. Game was also part of the summer diet: the hare was cooked in wine or stewed, and the partridge was prepared in various ways that enhanced its taste. The wild goat, with its rather tough meat, was cooked in a casserole and never on charcoals. The abundance of vegetables and greens in summer provide greater flexibility in meat recipes, although meat was consumed once a week (on Sundays). Meat is served with green beans, okras or garden produce, which Cretans occasionally preserve by air-drying.

The garden produce in summer offers the opportunity for the preparation of a variety of dishes. Courgette, eggplants, green peppers and other vegetables change to palatable dishes that are infused with the aromas of summer and the freshness of Cretan home gardens. There is indeed a wide range of ways in which these products are prepared. To make the renowned *gemistà* you will need the following ingredients: peppers, tomatoes and eggplants.

In summer, the *dolmàdes*, a term normally reserved for stuffed vine leaves, are made from courgette flowers and are relished by the Cretans. Picking courgette flowers from someone else's garden is allowed by common law, whereas the picking of other produce is a violation. The summer diet is simple, delectable and "perfumed" with the scents and images of the season.

The coming of autumn marks various changes in Cretan diet. The gardens enter a period of decline. At the plateau of Lassithi, the inhabitants cook a very tasty vegetarian meal with anything they can pick from their home gardens – the *sofagàda* (or *sympetheriò* in western Crete). Fruits abound during this season, conveying to the Cretan cuisine unique tastes. A lot of these fruits can be preserved to last through the cold winter period. In the past, Cretan households were stocked with grape-juice syrup, *Petimèzi*, raisins, dried figs or desserts made from autumn fruits, e.g. *Moustalevrià*. As autumn nudged on, the summer garden withered, but such winter produce as cauliflowers, celery and leeks offset the loss. *Lahanodolmàdes* are consumed both in autumn and winter. The cabbages in those seasons offer alternative but tasty solutions to meal preparations. For example, the celery and leeks are cooked in many ways. Autumn is a period of intensive farming, involving the toilsome picking of olives and the cultivation of land. These activities demand a frugal diet, which dried summer fruits and legumes can offer.

The diet of Cretans living in urban centres was not much different from the diet of others living in the hinterland of the island. Fresh garden produce at affordable prices has been available in town markets all year round for many years. In the past Crete had established trade relations with Alexandria of Egypt, Smyrna and Constantinople of Turkey, as well as with a number of coastal regions in Italy. Not many years ago, most urban families owned, and still do, a piece of farmland on the outskirts of town or at a nearby village (*metòhi*). This piece of farmland was a convenient source of fresh vegetables. Dairy producers, mainly from mountainous areas, would come to urban centres and sell their products themselves. In the beginning of the 20th century, there were a lot of traditional restaurants in the major towns of the island.

Their menus consisted mainly of homemade food cooked in virgin olive oil, in strict compliance with family practices all over the island, while food prepared to order (*tis òras*) was a rare case at that time.

Groups of Foodstuffs

Authoritative instructions in layman's terms about the kinds of food suitable for consumption are scientifically established and readily understood by consumers. However, references to specific ingredients (nutrients) are not practical for the average consumer, whose choice of foodstuff is mostly determined by the kind of foods and their origin, and not so much by their nutritional constituents.

Epidemiological studies associating nutrition with good health and prevention of diseases make references to specific foods for that matter.
The inclusion of a plethora of foodstuffs in our diet minimises the possibility of deficiency as to certain nutrients, the biological properties of which remain unknown even nowadays. Foodstuffs that are rarely recommended should not altogether be excluded from our diet, as they may be unique sources of one or more nutrients essential to man (e.g. vitamin B12 in meat).

In a common diet, no food should be regarded as harmful or even poisonous, unless the body is genetically predisposed to react to the intake of such food (e.g. broad beans in people with insufficiency in enzyme G 6 PD).

A. Cereals – Legumes

Minimally processed cereals are an excellent source of fibre, i.e. non-starchy polysaccharides. The term 'cereals' includes wheat, barley, rye, oats and rice, although the latter is not unanimously considered a cereal. In addition, other cereals are: the millet (a kind of corn), linseed, amaranth, buckwheat and Quinoa (a kind of rice). The latter is imported to Crete pre-packaged and immediate consumption.

A daily diet should include on average eight small servings of cereals or cereal products, including bread, preferably whole grain. This diet is a rich source of the vitamin B complex, invaluable minerals and hydrocarbons of slow absorption. Fibre has a positive influence on the lipid profile; it regulates diabetes mellitus and is recommended for constipation. Cretans have a long and loving relationship with bread. It all started in antiquity, when the wide and lush valleys of the island, as well as the terraced plots on mountainous areas, produced cereals of excellent quality. The Minoans had built storerooms where they hoarded large quantities of wheat.

Bread was not only a dietary staple for ancient Greeks, but a devotional item as well. In ancient times, there were various types of bread, made from water and honey or from olive oil and a special liquid – a mixture of honey and vinegar or wine.

In antiquity, there was a rich variety of bread, the result of various types of flour (wheat/corn or barley), kneading, shaping and baking practices.

The most common bread in antiquity was the one made from whole bran wheat or barley flour. Currently, we know of many bread recipes originating from the classical and Hellenistic periods. Ancient Greek bread names, indicative also of the way bread was baked, are the following:

- *Klivanìtes:* bread baked in furnaces (*klìvanos*)
- *Eskarìtes:* thin bread on the grill (*Skàra*)
- *Plitòs:* bread baked in a special receptacle filled with water.
- *Apopiriàs:* bread baked on charcoals
- *Alifalìtes:* bread brushed (*alìfo*) with olive oil during the baking process
- *Dipirìtes:* name given to bread by the Minoans who baked it twice to make it last longer. If we top it with cooked tomato, olive oil, *mizìthra* cheese, sea-salt and oregano, we get a very tasty bread, a light summer snack (currently Cretan *dàkos*).

As regards the shapes of bread in antiquity, we know of square, semicircular, concave and flat bread (*plakìtes*).

Dietary customs in the entire Byzantine Empire, which included Crete, were very much the same with those of classical Greece, also in terms of bread consumption and quality. The most

common bread during the long Byzantine period was the kivàrio: bread of lower quality made from a mixture of bran and flour.

The 'pure' bread from wheat flour sifted meticulously was the daily prerogative of the rich. The poor enjoyed this 'elite' bread only during festivities.

The Byzantines ate often roughly processed bread, e.g. *hiromilòpita* (flat bread from flour ground in millstones by hand) that was baked on a clay or metal plate or even on ashes (àthos), hence *athòpita* bread.

With bread involving a painstaking production process in the previous centuries, Cretans had a high regard for this staple. During the period of Turkish occupation, bread was usually made from coarse flour, mainly from barley, since according to the following saying: "Barley bread was the first creation of God." (Vlastos archive, v.37, p.12).

This saying highlights the importance ascribed to bread by Cretans. The preparation and baking of the barley bread, they used to say, requires a river and a forest to complete.

In other words, for the proper making and baking of barley bread one had to use large quantities of water and firewood, respectively. Barley bread was dried to convert to palatable rusks of various types: the *dàkos* type hard bread and barley rolls are most characteristic.

A representation on a sarcophagus found in the area of Agia Triàda in the valley of Messarà depicts a basket of bread next to a bird and the sacred tree of the Minoan period.

This shows the significance of bread in the daily diet of ancient Cretans.

The bread, made from the new crop of seeds, represents a most valuable offering of Cretans to the gods: a custom that survives in Greece to this day, drawing its origins from ancient Greece, when the Greeks made bloodless offerings or sacrifices to the gods. In the centuries that followed this practice was incorporated into Christian rituals – consecrated bread - and has survived to this day.

Other types of bread were prepared, and still are, on holidays, e.g. *Christòpsomo, Labrokouloùres*, and *Phanouròpites*, the latter offered on the feast of Agios Phanoùrios. The making and aesthetic value of this bread varied from one region to another. Decorations on bread added value and meaning to the end product. Bread decoration is an art and as such was practiced by experienced women, the *xobliàstres*, whose skills passed from one generation to the next and is still practiced by some old women in Crete.

Of equal significance is the ritual bread, the *àrtos* and the *pròsforo* (bread offerings). They had a relief representation on top (the result of pressing the dough with a large seal marking the offering). Other ritual bread was made for weddings and christenings or for relatives (fiancè, groom, best-man) and for guests. These bread items were magnificent works of art bearing representations in relief and a universe of symbols.

Furthermore, there are such bread products as must rolls, hard-bread nibbles, raisin-bread, ring-shaped bread, etc. The whole process, from sowing to reaping, from threshing to grinding to taking the bread hot out of the oven are of exceptional folkloric interest, as they carry with them age-old customs that have withstood the test of time.

Pasta is basically made from cereals and has been popular in Crete since Turkish occupation. Homemade pasta is consumed the same day it is made. Occasionally, Cretan women would make pasta and then air-dry it (never under the sun) and store it over a period of weeks or months.
This kind of food was light and healthy, preferred by farmers and townspeople alike.

Some areas on the island of Crete were renowned for their pasta preparations: simple to make and delicious in taste. Stone hand-mills used to be a requisite 'appliance' for all Cretan houses in the past. They were used in the production of many foods, and in the event a household ran out of bread, this age-old device provided an expedient and practical solution to flour making where the use of a wind- or water mill was a remote possibility.

Hand-mills are rarely found today. However, coarse wheat flour is available in the local markets, as well as electric appliances (mixers) that can produce this kind of flour. Nevertheless, wheat milled in a stone hand-mill is always the best. *Xinòhondros* is one of the most favourite dishes in Crete. It was made from crushed wheat in sour milk and was consumed either fresh or air-dried.

Finally, although some people classify potatoes and vegetables in the same foodstuff category, potatoes are more like processed cereals from a nutritional point of view. Potatoes, just as bread, have a high glycaemic index and modern nutrition experts recommend not more than 3 servings of potatoes per week.

Beans, lima beans, lentils, chickpeas, broad beans and split peas are all legumes. On average, 3 to 4 servings of legumes, combined with cereals (boiled or in bread form), should be consumed on a weekly basis. Legumes are hardly found on the menu in other European countries. However in Greece, legumes combine with olive oil to produce a wide variety of tasty dishes. Legumes incorporate some of the most beneficial effects of vegetables. Numerous medical reports claim that legumes protect the stomach from developing cancer. In addition, their glycaemic reactions are very mild. They are high in proteins and low in lipids, which increases their nutritional value. The Minoans offered legumes and vegetables to the gods, an act of "Thanks-Giving" in honour of those deities that made the earth bear its fruits in abundance. Some dietary customs of the ancient Cretans have survived to this day. For example, the boiling of all kinds of legumes once a year, and the consumption of the same by all the members of the family, including their livestock, is probably an ancient custom. The leftovers were placed on the roof of the house for the birds.

With the systematic cultivation of legumes and vegetables, man also organized systems of storage for his crops for periods of emergency, i.e. when the weather or sickness did not allow him to find fresh food in his environment.

In modern times, there are many ways to prepare meals with legumes. Since the ingredients of every meal in Crete were produced locally, Cretans combined meat and legumes of their own or local production. Notwithstanding their significance to health, these customs are also culturally significant.

The Cretans of the past centuries, even up until a few decades ago, were self-sufficient in farm and animal products. However, there was a great emphasis on the production and storage of legumes. Households in the country used to store their crop in special clay jars in their cellars.

B. Fruits-Vegetables-Greens

The Cretan diet prescribes approximately six servings of vegetables/greens and three servings of season fruit grown locally, at amounts enough to balance the average daily energy expenditure. Fruits, greens and vegetables are excellent sources of fibre, many micronutrients (potassium, calcium, vitamin C, vitamin B6, carotenoids, vitamin E, folic acid) as well as other elements with antioxidant qualities. Vegetables are either consumed in olive oil or raw in salads.

Greens (hòrta) mainly wild plants that are classified as vegetables, are part of the customary diet of the Greeks and are an excellent source of antioxidant substances.

Wild greens have played a significant role in our diet. There is a saying that describes the love of the Greeks for greens: "When the Greeks get fat, the donkeys die of starvation". This means that the Greeks have found good use of roots, leaves and seeds that are in abundance among the Greek flora.

Indeed, the flora of Crete is rich with edible plants and roots, a cheap source of food for all households. Through the centuries, the Cretans developed tight bonds with nature and plants. This relationship is represented in Minoan frescoes depicting a plethora of plants that played a significant role in the daily diet and cult practices.

The rich variety of local greens offered Cretans options for countless combinations and tastes. The same holds true for the methods of cooking them. It is of interest to note at this point that all greens and vegetables mentioned by Byzantine authors are still consumed in Crete today. In particular:

The mallow ('mòlochos' in Byzantium) is first boiled and then fried in whisked eggs. The dish is known as *sfougàto*.

The nettles, edible in antiquity and in the Byzantine period, are still consumed in various parts of the island, despite the fact that their hairs can cause irritation and itching when they come in contact with the skin. Other vegetables mentioned in Byzantine texts and edible in Crete today are: the sorrel, the wild amaranth, the sow thistle and many more. Scores of Cretan greens and herbs have been used in popular medicine for centuries, as they had in antiquity.

Most of the vegetables cultivated in ancient Greece are also cultivated in Cretan gardens today.

The Cretans of the past consumed a lot of greens and vegetables raw and are nowadays considered to be an integral part of an optimum diet. Modern Cretans remained faithful to this tradition, as greens are ever-present in salads and meals today.

The greens used raw in salads today are the following:

• **Spiny Chicory - "Stamnagàthi" (*Cichorium spinosum*):**
It was a medicinal plant for the ancient Greeks and Dioscurides informs us that it was much appreciated by the Cretans. It is consumed in oil and vinegar. Chicory is a thorny bush and its

name derives from an old practice of Cretans, who used this bush to cover the opening of water-crocks to stop insects from falling into the drinking water. The plethora of greens in Crete finds a colourful expression in an equal number of salads, which are the result of imagination and taste. Often, the chicory is mixed with other wild greens, spring onions (mainly the green part) and dill.

• **Chicory - "Radìki" (*Cichorium intybus*)**
The ancient Greeks appreciated it for its excellent nutritional and health benefits. Dioscurides makes note of its diuretic qualities and the Cretan Agàpios Monachos (Agàpios the Monk) says that this plant cleanses and cures the liver from every ailment. The leaves and root of this plant stimulate the appetite, help digestion, purify the blood and reduce fever. Because of its bitter taste the chicory is sprinkled with vinegar and consumed raw. It is usually mixed with other greens that offset its bitter taste.

The three main varieties of the cultivated chicory (*cichorium endivia*), commonly known as endive, are: the Belgian (or French) endive, the curly endive and escarole.

It is easy to find endives in most markets all year round. It contains a substance, intybin, which is responsible for the bitter taste but also an excellent tonic for the stomach.

• **Common Bright eyes - "Agalatsìda"** (*Reichardia picroides*)

This was known as 'galaktìs' by the Byzantines, 'galaktìda' in the Middle Ages and 'galatsìda' by modern Cretans.

The 4-letter prefix in Greek means milk, which inspired breast-feeding women to consume this herb in the false belief that it helped milk production. Its taste is mildly sweet.

• **Purslane - "Glistrìda"** (*Portulaca oleracea*)

It grows in the wild but is also cultivated in Crete to be used in salads during the summer period. The purslane makes delicious salads

as it is mixed with lettuce, tomatoes or cucumber. Because it is high in fatty substances that lower cholesterol levels, the purslane is considered a very healthy food.

Dioscurides claims that purslane cures headaches, stomach ulcers, spleen ailments and heartburn.

Research experts claim that the purslane is rich in linoleic acid, which is a significant factor for lower heart disease rates. The purslane is digested much easier if combined with garlic, arugula, basil, cress or other boiled greens.

• **Garden Peas - "Papoùles / Psarès / Kampiljès"** (*Pisum sativum*)

This vegetable is cultivated to be used mainly raw in salads. It has a mildly bitter taste. During the 40-day period of strict fasting at Easter, garden peas make an excellent fasting meal for Cretans.

It is consumed in olive oil and vinegar, and often sprinkled with salt but never with oil. In many areas of Crete garden peas, raw artichokes and salted black olives, are served with a local alcoholic drink, *tsikoudià*.

Wild greens and garden vegetables, as well as flour and olive oil, are the main ingredients for vegetable/herb pies.

Pies are a delicious expression of an age-old gastronomic tradition, constituting also the particular features of Greek nutrition. Pies are prepared in numerous versions, with such additional ingredients as cheese, eggs and milk. Herb pies, in particular, were frugal and practical meals that took little time to prepare, but offered a variety of tastes. They were served as a main dish or as snacks that farmers and shepherds would put in a bag or basket to take out in the fields or pasture and serve both as bread and as a main dish.

Pies, as a stand-alone Greek meal, are both tasty and cheap to make.

Greens used for pies are of two kinds: a) those used for principal stuffing, e.g. spinach, sorrel, amaranth, white beet, nettles, leeks, and b) those that lend particular taste and aroma, e.g. fennel, parsley, dill, mint, poppy, roman pimpernel, salsify, sow thistle, wild carrot, common plantain, ground ivy, vervain, etc.

Greens for pies are either used raw (chopped and hand-crushed), sprinkled with a fair amount of salt, or cooked with onions in olive oil. Small pies, the celebrated *kalitsoùnia*, are also customary in Crete, in contrast to large pies baked in large baking pans.

Greens suitable for kalitsounia pies:

• **Spinach - "Spanàki"** *(Spinacia oleracea)*
This is a well-known vegetable, without a particular taste but of excellent nutritional value, which marries well with other vegetables and greens, meat or seafood. It is a principal ingredient in pies and patties, such as *Bourèki*, and combines harmoniously with various soft and spicy cheeses, garlic and other condiments.

Spinach is rich in calcium. It contains iron, folic acid, vitamins C and K1, potassium and phosphorus. On account of its iron and vitamins (B9 and B12) spinach is recommended in cases of anaemia and fatigue. It lends a touch of colour on one's cheeks and, generally, helps people restore their blood levels following any loss of blood (menstruation, haemorrhage, surgery, etc.).

The phosphorus content in spinach is good for all those who carry out intellectual work, while its iron content, which purifies the blood, is beneficial to people who live in polluted urban centres.

Spinach should not be heated twice, as it may develop toxic, nitrous substances that are harmful to the body. In addition, because of its oxalic acid content, spinach is not recommended for the elderly, pregnant women and those suffering from rheumatism and arthritis.

• Sorrel - "Làpatha" *(Rumex)*

This plant is pleasantly sour. It is picked in winter and spring, mixed with other vegetables for pies or cooked with rice in soups. Its leaves are suitable for preparing *Dolmadàkia*, as an alternative to vine leaves. The Sorrel is used in making the French fricassee dishes or cooked with veal braised in tomato.

In popular medicine Sorrel is recommended for skin conditions (acne – abscesses), as well as to aid digestion. As it is high in oxalic acid, it must be used moderately by those suffering from rheumatisms, arthritis and renal ailments.

•Amaranth - "Vlìta" *(Amaranthus or Albersia)*

This amaranth offers a grassy and cool taste and is usually boiled with fresh, summer vegetables, e.g. vine leaves, potatoes, courgettes, carrots, beetroots, etc. It is also mixed with other greens in vegetable pies.

•White Beet - "Sèskoula" *(Beta vulgaris)*

The white beet has fairly large leaves that taste sweet. It is used just like spinach. In addition to vegetable pies, the white beet is cooked with codfish, black beans and lamb.

• **Nettles - "Tsouknìda"** *(Ultrica dioica)*
Dioscurides says that an infusion from nettles is an excellent diuretic and cathartic.

In addition, cataplasm from mashed nettle leaves is good for healing wounds. Nettles are rich in carotene B, which acts by way of preventing cancerous growths. As is the case with spinach, nettles are also recommended for treating fatigue and anaemia supporting the organism during the convalescence stage. Since they do not contain oxalic acid, nettles are also recommended for treating arthritis and rheumatisms. They are sweet in taste and in Southern Italy are used for the leavening of bread, to make cheese, curdled milk, but also mixed with other greens to make salads. Nettles are a natural laxative and improve sexual function. The histamine and formic acid in its leaves cause skin irritation and allergic reactions. To counteract this side effect, mallow leaves can be applied on the skin.

• **Leeks - "Pràssa"** *(Allium schoenoprasum)*
Leeks are rich in minerals, iron and vitamins. They make excellent tonic, antiseptic infusions and are antianemic. Leeks contain important oils that promote gastric functions and enhance the appetite. They grow in cool and wet environments from November to April. Wild leeks have a milder taste in relation to the other varieties and are sweeter than onions. This makes them ideal for vegetable pies, soups and delicate fish dishes. They are normally chopped with lettuce, radishes or sow thistle and used in salads. In accordance with tradition, Church chanters used to think very highly of leeks as they believed that their sweet constituents improved the tone of their voice.

• **Common fennel - "Màratho"** *(Foeniculum vulgare)*
The tender leaves and sprigs of fennel are collected from January to June, when the plant is in blossom. They are used to make fennel pies, marathòpites, and large vegetable pies cooked in baking pans. The ancient Greeks were very imaginative concerning fennel applications: they used them in preparing plakoùntas, a cake with nuts and honey, stuffed bread, sauces, legumes, etc. while the Roman bakers used fennel seeds to lend aroma to their bread.

Infusions from fennel seeds promote digestion and are ideal for treating flatulence and abdominal gas concentration.

Fennel seeds are mostly popular as a diuretic, a treatment for urine retention and swelling feet, ankles, hands, and eyelids. It is also believed that they contribute to the treatment of cellulite.

•Corn poppy - "Paparoùna" *(Papaver rhoeas)*

The green leaves of poppy are picked early in winter and used in omelettes, boiled or mixed with other greens, in meat dishes and certainly in pies.

Its petals are used for aromatic infusions and its seeds for pastries and bread. The oil from poppy seeds is good for invigorating the body and can treat constipation.

•Roman pimpernel or Mediterranean Hartwort - "Kafkalìthra" *(Tordylium apulum)*

It grows around the Mediterranean coasts but only in Greece has it found its way into the kitchen. We can come across 5-6 annual species that have almost the same taste and structure. They are very small with brittle, toothed and unequally divided leaves with an acute scent. This plant is known as 'Kafkalìthra' or 'Kafkalìda' in Peloponnese, Crete, the Ionian islands and Attica. Its name in Santorini is 'Agriokoutsounàda', in Kàssos 'Moskapidià', while in other areas it is known as 'Moskolàhano'. The Mediterranean hartwort is a principal ingredient in all spring pies made in Greece. It is also used in bean soups; it is cooked with kid's meat in an egg-lemon sauce (*avgolèmono*) and with codfish in casserole. The hartwort also fights bad breath.

•Shepherd's Needle - Ahàdjikas or Miròni *(Scandix pecten-veneris)*

This is a Mediterranean aromatic plant than can be picked from the end of winter to early spring, before it blossoms.

It is eaten raw, but also boiled, with meat, fish and legumes. It has a distinct taste and aroma, which makes it an ideal candidate for green pies, soups, salads and omelettes.

Dioscurides reports that it helps with the bowel movement; it also aids digestion and is diuretic. As an infusion, Dioscurides says that it also benefits the liver, the kidneys and the bladder.

•Salsify or Oyster Plant - Tragopògon (*Tragopogon porrifolius*)

Theophrastus called this plant 'Tragopogon', i.e. the beard of the billy-goat. Dioscurides, picking up from the bunch of the hair growing from the calyx of the Tragopògon, gave the plant the name '*kòmi*' meaning hair.
Modern Greek farmers gave it other names: 'beard of the hare', '*lagòhorto*' (hare's green), '*skoùlos*' or '*pigounìtis*'. French and American chefs make good use of Tragopògon but also refer to it as oyster plant or salsily. Its can be found almost everywhere in Greece.
Its leaves are lance-shaped and very similar to the leeks'. People pick its tender leaves from January to March, when not yet fully grown. They are mixed in small quantities with other greens and make delicious pies.
In Europe, particularly in France, the plant is mainly cultivated exclusively for its white roots, which are collected in spring to make soups with an oyster-like taste.

•Sow thistle - "Zòchos" (*Sonchus oleraceus*)

Its most common names are Zòhos, Tsòhos, Ntsòhos or Galatsìda. It is best picked when still not fully grown, when its sprigs are tender and milky in texture, with leaves pleasant in taste.
It is used in various salads, pies and is boiled with other greens to offset its bitter taste. The sow thistle is very common in Greece. It was also used to counteract scorpion bites.

plant's qualities as follows: "From other plants only the sprigs can be used, but from the wild carrot one can also use the root, which can be accompanied with wine." Dioscurides also mentions the Cretan stafilìnakas, saying that "the carrot by the Cretan name bears leaves similar to the fennel".

He goes on to add that "its flowers are white and its fruits, if chewed, sharp in taste and very aromatic. As for its root, it is roughly as thick as a human finger."

• **Wild carrot or Daucus - "Stafilìnakas"** *(Daucus carota)*

It is cultivated as a vegetable with such names as Karòto, Dafkì, Pastinàka, Bastinàka, Havoùtsi, Moskorèpano, Kavoùtsi, Stafilòni and Voùtsi. The modern carrot evolved from this wild species. Stafilìnakas is the wild, ancient Greek carrot with a white root and an intoxicating aroma.

The tender sprigs and leaves of this plant have a pungent taste and scent that can be applied to a mixture of greens for pies.

In Hios the plant is known as trahanòhorto, since the women of the island treated trahanàs with it to make a delicious soup. They first air-dried and then rubbed the wild carrot with the frumenty. Dioscurides describes the

• **Common Plantain - "Pentànevro, Arnòglosso"** *(Plantago)*

It can be found anywhere in Greece, grows in wet locations and produces five large and sinewy leaves, hence its name Pentànevro. Its leaves, picked from December to July, have a mild taste and are rather sweet and refreshing. They are used in moderation with other greens and can be boiled or used in pies.

In Europe and mainland Greece, the Pentànevro is used for making an infusion, while in Crete it is mixed with edible wild greens.

Tradition says that this plant cures the five "veins" of people, i.e. diseases related to the senses.

This is a medicinal plant and was used by country folk for treating insect bites and slow healing wounds.

•Ground Ivy - "Glèhoma or Glìhoma" *(Glechoma hederacea)*

It prefers cool and shady environments, particularly under locust trees and in lentisk bushes. Because of its aromatic taste, it often replaces parsley in meals. This plant is also known as 'lagoudopaxìmado' or 'glèhoma' and looks like ivy, a similarity not only in name, but also in form.

•Vervain - "Gorgogiànnis, Vèrvena, Ierovotàni *(Verbena officinalis)*

Vervain is known in popular medicine as stavrovòtano, stamatòhorto, wild louiza and gorgogiànis. The name stamatòhorto suggests the quality of this plant to help stop haemorrhaging.

The compound name gorgogiànnis (gorgòs =fast, giànis>igièno = to cure) also describes one of the plant's qualities. It gives an odourless extract, rather bitter in taste, which is widely used in the treatment of various ailments.

In Europe and mainland Greece, this plant is used for making an infusion, while in Crete it is mixed with edible wild greens mainly for its medicinal qualities. There is a popular saying, extracted from a 15th century text, which illustrates the plant's therapeutic applications:

"Gorgogiànnis is my name and am a popular weed,

and those who boil and drink of me, their pains I relieve".

Dioscurides calls this plant Ierà Votàni and Peristèreon Òrthios. The vervain has been a medicinal plant since antiquity. The ancient Greeks ascribed to it magical qualities and used to devote it to the Druids, the nymphs of the forests.

Other greens used frequently in the Cretan Diet:

•**Black Bryony - Avroniès** *(Tamus communis)*

Dioscurides says that its shoots on first bloom, if boiled and consumed, are a powerful diuretic and also enhance the intestinal functions. Today Cretans consume large quantities of black bryony, which they either boil and then serve in olive oil and vinegar, mix it with garlic to reduce its bitter taste, or use it in omelettes, even in seafood.

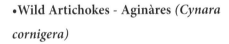

•**Wild Artichokes - Aginàres** *(Cynara cornigera)*

Artichokes were not cultivated in ancient Greece, but found in the wild and were much appreciated by the ancients.

In the past, the whitish-green leaves of the wild artichoke were cooked with young goat's meat. The flowers of the wild artichoke are eaten in the same way as those of the cultivated species. They are delicious food, rich in calcium and vitamins (A, B1, B2, C). When raw, the flowers marry well with olives, broad beans, *dàkos* and served with *tsikoudià*, the traditional Cretan alcohol distillate. Artichokes are a remedy for kidney diseases. In popular medicine they were used for their diuretic and anti-anemic qualities.

•**Golden Thistle - "Askòlibro"** *(Scolymus hispanicus)*

Dioscurides says that only its tender stem was edible, which grows much like those of asparagus. It is collected in winter or beginning of spring. Its edible parts today are the leaves, skin and roots. In popular medicine the golden thistle, particularly the juice from its boiled roots, was used to treat kidney stones, arthritis, etc. The golden thistle is boiled and cooked in *avgolèmono* sauce with fish, meat, snails and in omelettes. Although a thistle, it was much preferred in Crete.

• Tassel Hyacinth - "Volvì" *(Muscari comosum)*

Dioscurides reports that the Tassel Hyacinth is good for the stomach and can alleviate pain in the joints. It was believed that if you boil the bulbs and sprinkle them with olive oil, vinegar and thyme, they can enhance male virility. This belief describes the general ancient Greek attitude to bitter bulbs, which ascribed to them aphrodisiac qualities.

The bulbs, pink or white in colour, are usually picked in spring. The magnificent pinkish bulbs can constitute an excellent appetizer. However, the white bulbs are sweeter. In general, the bulbs of this plant can be preserved for months in glass jars.

• Asparagus - Sparàgia *(Asparagus sp.)*

Asparagus offers a mild, sweet taste and is mainly used in soups and omelettes, as hors-d'oeuvres and in meat cooked in *avgolèmono* sauce.

The wild asparagus is very tasty and we can find it in the wild or in cultivated plots.

Cultivated asparagus is good for the blood and stomach; it is an excellent aphrodisiac and a very healthy food, in general. The heads of this plant are rich in magnesium, phosphorus and vitamins. The asparagus contains asparagine, an amino acid that promotes physical growth and multiplication and regeneration of the body cells. There are many species of wild asparagus and only three species of the cultivated variety (white, purple, and green). The white species are fleshy and commercially canned. The green asparagus, cultivated in France, is crunchy and also canned. The asparagus is delicious when sprinkled with virgin olive oil and lemon or vinegar. It is also used in omelettes or can stand alone baked in the oven or cooked over charcoal.

• Bracken Fern - "Ftères" *(Pteridium aquilinum)*

The Bracken Fern is a flowerless plant. Before its tender shoots turn into leaves they can be picked and made into a delicious meal. To make an omelette out of them, you first need to boil them a little. Alternatively, you can dip the leaves in a thick flour batter and fry them in olive oil.

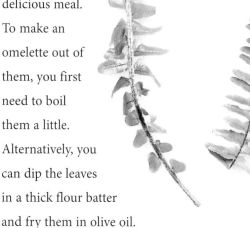

C. Oil – Olives

The history of olives and olive oil and the history of Crete are intricately woven in the fabric of time, from the remote past, when Crete became the cradle of western civilization and marked the historical course of Europe.

Based on archaeological finds, many historians believe Crete to be the home of the olive tree. Scientific reports claim that olive trees were initially cultivated in Crete in 3000 BC. A primitive oil press has been found in one of the main halls of the palace at Knossos. The oil press was fixed with pipes that carried the olive oil to gigantic pìthi (clay jars).

According to classical Cretan mythology, Athena was born on Crete, near the springs of river Triton. The olive tree is her gift to the people of Crete. Similarly, Dactylus Hercules introduced the cultivation of olive trees to the people of the Peloponnese. With olive trees playing a significant role in cult practices on the island, they were revered and protected. This explains why the olive is considered holy and managed to survive on the island through the centuries to ultimately become the main source of income for Cretans.

Nevertheless, both the ancient Egyptians and the Palestinians were familiar with the cultivation of olive trees. Oil production in Crete was in the form of established enterprises in settlements, in palaces and in the mansions of landowners. Initially, olive oil production on the island covered domestic needs, but later Minoans exported oil to mainland Greece and the Cyclades.

The nutritional value of olive oil, the fact that it promotes health, has been common knowledge since ancient times. Such celebrated physicians of antiquity as Hippocrates (father of medicine), Galen and Dioscurides extolled the merits of olive oil. For the Greeks, the olive was a symbol for peace, wisdom, victory, fertility, religion, fine arts and noble sports. With the passing of centuries the effects of olive oil in physical health, spiritual and intellectual well-being spread all over the world.

The fact that ancient Cretans were familiar with the cultivation of olive trees has been established through archaeological findings, organic residues, facilities and tools for the pressing of olives, tables and inscriptions with references to olive trees and olive oil. Paul Faure reported that during the Minoan period the average Cretan farmer not only considered the olive tree important, but almost holy, not only for its edible products

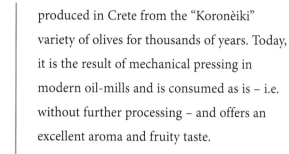

- olives and olive oil - but also because he used the olive olive oil in body-care products and for medicinal purposes. Furthermore, the olive oil was used in cult practices, in magic, for practical purposes (lubricant, combustion, lighting), in sports and in post-mortem care of the deceased.

At some point in the remote past, the olive tree made Crete its home, an ideal habitat in the middle of the Mediterranean. The olive tree prefers mild climates, where winters are not as biting and sunlight is profuse. It grows better on fertile soils, but it will do just as well on barren land – dry and rocky landscape that makes up most parts of the island. Today there are approximately 30 million olive trees in Crete, in the loving care of 95 thousand families.

The climatic conditions that prevail on the island, as well as the soil, are a significant factor for the quality of olive oil produced locally. Cretan olive oil, this magnificent juice with an exceptional aroma, pleasant taste and highly nutritious value, has been celebrated worldwide and has won numerous distinctions and awards. The extra virgin Cretan olive oil is as precious as gold and should be used in daily meals. It is the fresh juice extracted from olives with a low acidity level ranging from 0.1 - 0.8%. It has been

produced in Crete from the "Koronèiki" variety of olives for thousands of years. Today, it is the result of mechanical pressing in modern oil-mills and is consumed as is – i.e. without further processing – and offers an excellent aroma and fruity taste.

Production

Olive oil is the result of:

• excellent soil and climatic conditions that lend Crete its unique character (long periods of sunshine during the year, mild winters and cool summers, the mountainous and hilly bas-relief, fertile soil and clean environment),

• the love, care and accumulated knowledge of farmers who love olive oil and respect the environment.

Biological, nutritional, medicinal properties of olive oil

In terms of benefits to man, extra virgin olive oil is the undisputable champion among fatty substances known today.

This is corroborated by numerous research results, the outcomes from scores of epidemiological studies around the world, and by the long experience of Cretans who have been committed to an extra virgin olive oil diet for centuries.

The paradigm of the Cretan Diet has made significant impact in the western world and has found earnest followers.

Extra Virgin Olive Oil promotes physical well-being and shields people from numerous diseases.

In particular:

•It is recommended against gastrointestinal and kidney diseases

•It mitigates the development of cholelithiasis

•It can provide relief to patients suffering from diabetes

•It protects the skin from harmful sun rays

•It is beneficial to the growth of the human frame

•It promotes youth

•It obstructs the development of cardiovascular diseases and numerous cancers.

The ancient Greeks believed that virgin olive oil provided health benefits and was used:

•to treat skin diseases

•as an emetic (to induce vomiting)

•in the care of wounds and burns

•to treat ear infections

•in gynaecological diseases

•as a birth control option

According to the Hippocratic Code, olive oil was considered beneficial for more than 60 ailments:

Use: Extra virgin olive oil is used raw in salads, or cooked, to produce delicious and healthy meals.

It certainly is better than other fatty substances and should be used to replace them.

It is quite resistant to high temperatures (in frying).

Although fatty substances tend to infiltrate foods during frying, this is not the case with extra virgin olive oil, at least not to a significant degree. Consequently, food fried in olive oil is digested better. Even if you heat the virgin olive oil in 200°C it retains its bile secretory and conductive properties and is also beneficial for the liver, thus promoting the metabolism of lipids.

Daily Regime: the quantity of olive oil recommended for daily consumption must meet the requirements of the body for fatty acids at a level of 10% - 15%. Consequently, if the body needs 2,500 calories per day, then 25-35 grams of olive oil per day should suffice to provide the required amounts of fatty acids and vitamin E.

When the Body Mass Index (BMI: the ratio of body weight in kilograms to the square of height in metres) is at 25kg/m^2, there is no scientific evidence to support the claim that one should reduce the intake of olive oil, despite its high energy content. Increasing physical activity and reducing the intake of calories are priorities in any good weight-loss diet. Foodstuffs do not change one's BMI other than through their energy content. Reducing olive oil intake should not be considered a wise option when this involves reductions in vegetables and legumes, which are mainly cooked in olive oil.

Nutritional Value:

(per 10gr of olive oil: equivalent to a full tablespoon)

Calories (CAL)	90
Proteins (gr)	0
Carbohydrates (gr)	0
Fats (gr)	10
Cholesterol (mg)	0
Sodium (mg)	0
Vitamin E (mg/100gr)	15-25
Provitamin A (mg/100gr)	1-4
Fatty compounds per 10gr	
Monounsaturates (gr)	7.6
Polyunsaturates (gr)	1
Saturates (gr)	1.4

Consumption of olive oil in Greece is approximately 2,000 tons/year, which corresponds to 75% of average annual domestic production and to 15% of the EU average rate of consumption annually.

Per capita consumption of olive oil in Greece is at 20kg/year, which is the highest in the world. In some areas of Crete, it is even higher, reaching 34kg per capita annually. The corresponding rate for the rest of Greece is 17.5kg.

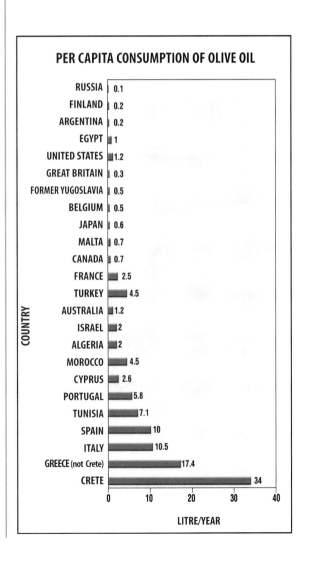

PER CAPITA CONSUMPTION OF OLIVE OIL

COUNTRY	LITRE/YEAR
RUSSIA	0.1
FINLAND	0.2
ARGENTINA	0.2
EGYPT	1
UNITED STATES	1.2
GREAT BRITAIN	0.3
FORMER YUGOSLAVIA	0.5
BELGIUM	0.5
JAPAN	0.6
MALTA	0.7
CANADA	0.7
FRANCE	2.5
TURKEY	4.5
AUSTRALIA	1.2
ISRAEL	2
ALGERIA	2
MOROCCO	4.5
CYPRUS	2.6
PORTUGAL	5.8
TUNISIA	7.1
SPAIN	10
ITALY	10.5
GREECE (not Crete)	17.4
CRETE	34

Greek olive oil, as is produced today, has an acidity level lower than 1% with organoleptic characteristics that qualify it as EXTRA VIRGIN OLIVE OIL in quantities ranging from 85% - 95% of total national production. Naturally, these estimates depend on the weather conditions of a particular season. The corresponding percentages of other oil producing countries (Italy, Spain) are lower.

The basic factors contributing to the excellent quality of Greek olive oil are: the effective treatment of diseases affecting olive trees, especially the olive fly (*Dacus oleae*), the short period between harvest and crushing of the fruit and the sanitary conditions observed in groves, oil mills and the standardization facilities/production.

Cutting short the period (currently to 1-2 days) from harvest to crushing during the last few years has been achieved by mechanical means (small mechanical harvesters) and the modernization of the high capacity Greek oil mills.

In spite of the fact that the International Olive Oil Council (IOOC) and the EU have acknowledged the top quality of Greek olive oil, most consumers have been unable to distinguish between **'virgin olive oil'** and common **'olive oil'**. The difference between the two is very significant.

On the basis of the current official olive oil classification standards, virgin olive oil is oil extracted from the fruits of olive trees exclusively by mechanical or natural means under low thermal conditions. It follows, then, that olive oil is a natural juice that retains intact all the basic substances of the olive fruit (vitamins, trace elements, etc.), which render it beneficial to man.

Virgin olive oil, depending on its acidity level, is distinguished as follows: Extra virgin olive oil with an acidity not exceeding 0.8%; virgin olive oil with an acidity of not more than 1.5%; lampante virgin of an acidity higher than 2% rendering it unfit for direct consumption, unless it is processed.

Finally, **'Refined Olive Oil'** and **'Olive Oil'** represent olive oil obtained from **'Virgin Olive Oil'** by refining methods and is usually referred to as pure!

However, the term 'Refined Olive Oil' or 'Olive Oil' is not informative enough to let consumers understand that the particular types contain significant amounts of olive oil that have been processed by chemical means.

Of course, it should be noted at this point that all vegetable oils from various seeds (corn, sunflower, soy, etc.), usually referred to as seed-oils, are the result of some chemical process or other.

In addition to the acidity (oleic acid) levels and the absorbance readings from spectroscopic ultraviolet investigation, other olive oil parameters should be checked, e.g. the superoxide index and wax content.

The aforementioned analyses of olive oil are required by EEC Regulation No. 2568/91, as amended by the Commission Regulation (No. 1019/2002) dated June 13th, 2002, and lay down the marketing standards for olive oil, as they come under the Commission Directive No. 1989/2003/EC dated November 6th, 2003 in accordance with which all aforementioned parameters certifying olive oil quality should be appropriately indicated on all types of labelling.

OLIVE OIL CHARACTERISTICS						
CATEGORY	ACIDITY (%)	SUPEROXIDE INDEX mEq O2/kg	WAX mg/kg	K232	K270	DELTA-K
VIRGIN OLIVE OIL	≤0.8	≤20	≤250	≤2,50	≤0.22	≤0.01
EXTRA VIRGIN OLIVE OIL	≤2.0	≤20	≤250	≤2.60	≤0.25	≤0.01
LAMPANTE	>2.0	-	≤300	-	-	-
REFINED OLIVE OIL	≤0.3	≤5	≤350	-	≤1.10	≤0.16
MIX OF REFINED OLIVE OILS AND VIRGIN OLIVE OILS	≤1.0	≤15	≤350	-	≤0.90	≤0.15
Crude olive residue oil	-	-	≥350	-	-	-
Refined olive-residue oil	≤0.3	≤5	>350	-	≤2.00	≤0.20
Olive-residue oil	≤1.0	≤1.5	>350	-	≤1.70	≤0.18

In addition, the following should also appear on packaging:

a. For extra virgin olive oil: "superior-category olive oil obtained directly from olives and solely by mechanical means."

b. For virgin olive oil: "Olive oil obtained directly from olives and solely by mechanical means"

c. For olive oil: "Oil comprising exclusively olive oils that have undergone refining and oils obtained directly from olives."

The designation of origin on the label is also required exclusively for extra virgin olive oil. According to the new regulation, this designation of origin refers to the geographical location where the oil has been produced and the name of the location must be mentioned on the label or packaging.

The Ministry of Agriculture and the European Union recognise that olive oil produced in the entire prefecture of Hania meets the "Protected Geographical Indication (PGI)" criteria. Moreover, in order to qualify for a PGI designation, olive oil must be registered with the Ministry of Agriculture and be stored appropriately so as to ensure the PGI designation.

Also, the indication "first cold-pressing" is only for extra virgin olive oil and virgin olive oil taken during a thermal process involving a temperature lower than 27°C and a first mechanical pressing of the olive-pomace in a traditional system of extraction by means of hydraulic presses.

The indication "cold extraction" is only for extra virgin olive oil and virgin olive oil taken at lower than 27°C by way of infiltration or centrifugation of the olive-pomace. Lastly, the indications for the organoleptic characteristics of olive oil may appear on labels only if the relevant organoleptic tests comply with EEC Regulation 2568/91.

The implementation of Commission Regulation (EC) No. 1019/2002 became mandatory for Greece in 2005. This is because the oils that had been produced and packaged before June 13, 2002 had a shelf life of 2 years.

One can find a lot of scientific (including medical) documentation about olive oil on the Internet at: http://europa.eu.int/olive-oil. As regards the metabolism of the lipids we can quote the following:

"Hyperlipidemia, smoking and high blood pressure are some of the risk factors associated with coronary heart disease (CHD). Of these risk factors, 'cholesterol' is particularly important. It is now understood that there are two types of cholesterol – low-density lipoprotein (LDL) and high-density lipoprotein (HDL) – the so-called 'bad' and 'good' cholesterol respectively. High levels of HDL cholesterol reduce CHD risk, whereas increased levels of LDL cholesterol increase CHD risk.

In the Western diet the three saturated fatty acids (SAFAs), i.e. lauric (e.g. palm kernel oil, coconut oil), myristic acid (e.g. butter, coconut oil) and palmitic acid (e.g. animal fat) comprise 60-70% of all SAFAs and are responsible for the cholesterol-rising effect of saturated fat.

To maintain a balance in energy intake-output, a common strategy is to reduce the SAFAs in the diet and replace it with polyunsaturated fatty acids (PUFAs), e.g. sunflower oil or monounsaturated fatty acids (MUFAs), e.g. oleic acid, which is the predominant fat in olive oil.

The MUFAs are more resistant to oxidation in comparison to the PUFAs of seed oils. The oxidation of the polyunsaturated fatty acids is responsible for atheromatic changes and the development of cancer."

Olive oil is rich in monounsaturated acids, important in the constitution of lipids, which supply human cells energy, the "building blocks" of our organism. Olive oil has a positive effect on the growth and development of the human organism and counteracts the aging process as it offers large amounts of vitamin E. It reduces cholesterol levels and mitigates the hardening of the walls of arteries, atherosclerosis, which is the main cause of death in industrial countries.

On the basis of scientific research the cholesterol levels in blood and the risk from Coronary Disease (CD) are much lower in Mediterranean countries in relation to other countries.

Olive oil is very effective in treating peptic ulcers and its consumption relieves one from abdominal pain and reduces occurrences of indigestion after meals.

As early as a century ago it was established that such supplementary food as pulp with olive oil reduces gastric secretions.

It helps the liver; relieves one from the annoying contractions of the gallbladder and obstructs the formation of stones in the bile. It also relieves one from atonic constipation and acts as a mild cathartic. Olive oil has a significant role in the treatment of diabetes. On the basis of recent research in the USA, women who consumed olive oil more than once a day manifested 25% less cancer of the breast, since olive oil does not favour chemically related tumours, in contrast to other types of oil. It is remarkable that olive oil has been associated with a wide range of health benefits and is recommended among others for diabetes mellitus. The beneficial effects of olive oil in the latter disease result from olive oil's monounsaturated acid content, as well as its plethora of antioxidant agents, which are mainly found in the extra virgin variety.

This scientific evidence as regards the health benefits of olive oil is sufficient to warrant the launching of a strategic campaign with the aim of mobilizing people with political leverage, health practitioners, educators, dieticians, the mass media and school canteen suppliers in promoting the principles of the Mediterranean Diet on a national and international scale.

Owing to their constituent elements, olives are an excellent nutritional supplement for man. Their average energy content is higher than that of other fruits and vegetables. Olives offered at our tables contain: olive oil, proteins with all their principal amino acids, sugars, tannins, steroid glycoside, cerebrosides, and sulphuric stone.

The inorganic content of the olive fruit, also beneficial to man, includes: iron, calcium, magnesium, phosphorus, etc. Actually, its calcium content is much higher in comparison not only to fruits and vegetables, but also to meat, fish, bread and other foodstuffs, and equals that of cow's milk. In addition, olives are rich in vitamin A.

Following the above information, one can hardly doubt the benefits of olives for man. Consequently, it is an invaluable supplement and should be consumed more often. A number of diet experts recommend 80 grams of olives per day.

D. Wine

Wine has been consumed since ancient times. For thousands of years, wine has been an indispensable accompaniment to food all around the Mediterranean. Considering its nutritional value, one could classify wine as food, but it should be consumed in moderation, as is the case for all kinds of food.

Hippocrates prescribed remedies most of which contained wine.
Later, Heberden (1786) recommended wine in the treatment of heartburn.
In his book about heart diseases (1951), the physician of Eisenhower, Dr. Paul D. White, and father of modern cardiology, claimed that the most effective medication in the treatment of heartburns, second only to nitrates, is alcohol in moderate amounts. Other studies, e.g. the Framigham Study (Gordon, 1983) and that of Eric Rimm (Harvard, 1991), concluded that alcohol is beneficial only, if taken systematically in moderate amounts.

Consumption of up to four glasses per day reduces mortality rates from CHD from 15 - 60% in relation to those who abstain from wine completely. However, consumption in excess of 4 glasses is associated with decreased protection against CHD.
Serge Renaud, professor of cardiology, claimed in a public broadcast in France that alcohol is one of the most effective drugs in reducing the likelihood of coronary heart disease.

Consumption of alcoholic drinks in amounts equalling 30gr and 15 gr of ethyl alcohol a day by men and women respectively is beneficial to their health. There is evidence to support the claim that wine consumption during meals is more beneficial than liqueur or beer outside meals.

Consumption of four glasses and two glasses of wine per day by men and women respectively has positive effects on their health.
There is no doubt that excessive amounts of ethyl alcohol increases or exacerbates morbidity and social concerns. Alcoholism is a major problem for modern societies. However, we should make a distinction between wine and other alcoholic beverages. It is true that wine contains alcohol, but its consumption is actually not intended to induce inebriation, or meet the needs of an alcohol addict.

There is a certain form of cancer that is associated with smoking and alcohol – the cancer of the oral cavity and pharynx (stomatopharyngeal cancer). The risk for this cancer increases, when excessive amounts of alcohol are consumed.

However, the risk decreases by 20% - 50% with up to four glasses of wine per day. In conclusion, wine is the only alcoholic drink which, taken in moderation, protects man from cancer of the oral cavity and pharynx.
Many people claim that red wine is healthier than other varieties of wine, e.g. white wine.

This claim is probably based on the colour of red wine, which is the result of tannins, phenolic compounds with antioxidant substances. Thrombin, an enzyme the accumulation of which creates blood clots, is formed with the oxidation of fatty substances in the blood plasma. It has been proven that tannins in red wine reduce the production of all lipid superoxides, thus preventing the accumulation of thrombin in blood and subsequent blood clotting.

On the basis of recent research by the National Heart & Lung Institute of the Imperial College of London, red wine is also beneficial in cases of Chronic Obstructive Lung Disease (COLD). The vegetable polyphenols, e.g. resveratrol, which are in high concentration in red wine, combat the inflammation of the lungs in cases of COLD.
It has been proven that phenol extractions in red wine obstruct the oxidation of low-density lipoproteins (LDL), much more effectively than vitamin E (Frankel et al, 1993).

The superoxidation of lipids is a phenomenon implicated in CHD, cancer growth and aging. The inhibition of the superoxidation of lipids, attained by moderate amounts of wine intake, increases longevity and boosts health. Dr. David Sinclair and his colleagues at the Harvard Medical School claim that the secret of maintaining one's youth or, even better, extending one's youth, is locked in the vegetable polyphenols which activate the sirtuin enzyme. This enzyme inhibits the apoptosis (death of cells) process and, thus, mitigates aging of the cells. According to Dr. Sinclair, the activated enzyme protects cells and allows them to survive longer, in spite of their "wear and tear" over the years.

In addition, wine is an excellent accompaniment to meals.
When at lunch and dinner we take a moderate amount of wine, we become more cheerful, enjoy our food and benefit from it more. Otherwise, we tend to eat fast, having no mood to stay longer at the table, in which case we have failed to enjoy our food and might also develop indigestion.

It has been a long tradition on Crete, and has passed down on record, that a farmer starts his day with a good, traditional breakfast, which includes a glass of wine. The "*akràtisma*" of the ancient Greeks, i.e. the dipping of barley rusk in a glass of wine, has probably evolved into this breakfast tradition of the Cretan farmers. Cretan farmers have a mid-day snack in the fields, olive groves and vineyards, which includes the second glass of wine of the day. The third glass follows during a frugal lunch at home or on the field.

Clay jars, dating from ca. 2200 BC, were unearthed from the Early-Minoan settlement of *Mirtos* in Crete. Chemical analysis of residues in the jars points to a wine laced with resin (Retsìna wine). These findings are solid proof of wine's ancient use and consumption in ancient Greece. Similar residues were found in a false-neck amphora (stirrup jar) discovered in the Mycenaean palace, which proves that during the Copper Age people knew about resinated wine. There is further solid evidence of distilled alcoholic drinks in the Middle-Minoan period (1900-1700 BC.)
Could the famous local drink of modern Cretans, *tsikoudià*, derive its origin from ancient alcohol making practices? We tend to believe so, as Cretans are people who respect old customs and tradition, which they pass down a long chain of generations.

Tsikoudià is a drink tied with another age-old tradition of Cretans – hospitality. Cretans treat their guests with homemade snacks and a small glass of *tsikoudià* on the side.

E. Honey

Honey is the sweet viscous substance made by worker bees from the nectar of flowers or from the excretions of the insects of coniferous trees. The flower honey is named after the plant, the nectar of which is used by workers to produce the honey. There is, for instance, thyme, acacia, heather honey, etc.

Its chemical composition depends on the type of flower, the climatic conditions dominating in the production areas, as well as the standardization method employed when traded.

Blossom honey (flower honey) consists of 15% - 20% water, 80% hydrocarbons, predominantly glucose, fructose with sucrose and maltose, as well as 0.4% albumens. It contains organic acids (malic, citric, gluconic acids), enzymes (amylase, catalase, invertase) aromatic and inorganic substances (K, Na, Ca), vitamins (B2, PP, C, B6, N, K and E), alkaloids and pigments.

The colour depends on the flowers of the plant from which the nectar has been collected. Therefore, acacia honey is yellow coloured; thyme honey is light amber; heather honey is dark amber, etc. Its aroma and taste depend on its origin.

The consistency of honey varies: acacia honey is very fluid to watery, thyme honey is viscous, the honey of conifers is even more viscous, while heather honey crystallizes fast.

Its nutritional and therapeutical value has been recognised by all people since ancient times. This is why honey has been established as a staple food for humans having a nutritional value as equal to that of milk.

Honey was the main food of the philosophers Democritus and Diogenes. In antiquity "*melikraton*" and ambrosia were regarded as the best drink for humans and Gods respectively and both were made of honey and milk.

Saint John the Baptist, lived on green and shoot tops, as well as honey from wild bees.

Honey production in Crete dates back to prehistoric times.

One of the most important exhibits in the museum of Heraklion, the museum where many secrets of the Minoan civilisation are kept, is a wonderful golden jewel representing two bees that provides proof of the relationship between Cretan people and bees since antiquity.

Cretan honey constitutes an excellent, natural product with a distinctive aroma due to the exceptionally rich variety of aromatic plants predominant on the island.

F. Aromatic plants and herbs

Aromatic plants or herbs are used extensively in Crete not only for their aroma and taste but also for their medicinal properties. They are included in recipes for meals, pastries and drinks, or used in the form of infusions, decoctions and cataplasms. Furthermore, they can serve as active agents in aromatic, cosmetic or cleansing products. Anthropological and botanical studies in Crete in the recent past ascertained that local herbs are part of the customary diet of Cretans, but also used for medicinal purposes. These herbs have been known since ancient times and there is ample evidence regarding their medicinal applications. This information comes from archaeological excavations at Knossos and the texts of Theophrastus and Dioscurides.

In addition to the strong relationship he established between proper nutrition and diseases, Hippocrates, the father of medicine, insisted that all food intended for consumption should be healthy and a source of pleasure. The latter is achieved by adding to food the right amount of herbs, which are rich in antioxidants and can replace salt. Moreover, herbs can add flavour to foods and provide a feeling of satiety preventing, thus, overeating.

Disclaimer: The information contained in the following brief descriptions of herbs that are part of the Cretan flora is provided to the reader only for information purposes and not as a recommendation for the herbs in relation to their medicinal qualities. Prior to using these herbs, one should consult their physician.

• **Couch grass - "Agriàda"** (*Agropyron repens*)
Useful parts: rhizomes.
It grows invariably in fields and gardens throughout Greece and is a real "pest" for gardeners and farmers alike. However, it is a very interesting plant for botanists. Its rhizomes are collected in summer and have mild diuretic and antibiotic qualities, ideal for the human urinary system.

The agropyrene, derived from the volatile oil of the couch grass, has excellent antibiotic qualities. It is also a diuretic, dissolves the stones in kidneys and treats inflammation of the bladder.

It is a soothing diuretic, calming pain and spasm in the urinary tract, in addition to its positive effects in the treatment of rheumatism and cellulite.

Infusion: 1 cup warm or cold drink before each meal.

• Angelica - "Agelikì" *(Angelica archangelica)*

Useful parts: seeds, petioles, roots

According to local legends, this plant was named after an angel who revealed to a monk the positive effects of the plant in the treatment of plague.

It offers an aromatic flavour and cures the stomach from indigestion, colic pain and gas. Angelica is also good for coughs, asthma and bronchitis. It contains a substance, pinine, whose volatile oil has antimicrobial and expectorant properties. In addition, angelica is a diuretic and antiseptic, hence effective in the treatment of infections of the urinary system.

Its leaves enhance appetite and can be

mixed with fruit or fish. Infusion: 1 warm cup causes perspiration and it is good for colds.

• Dill - "Ànithos" *(Anethum graveolens)*

Useful parts: Overground parts

It originated from the East to later spread to the entire Mediterranean basin, and currently grows wild in fields and plots. It is also cultivated for its flavour and, according to the ancient Greek comedian Alexis (ca. 375 – ca. 275), it is a spice that chefs should not do without.

It is used in many medicinal preparations for children as it relieves flatulence and colic pain. The dill's seeds and leaves make an excellent tonic and have diuretic and antispasmodic qualities. It finds excellent culinary applications, stimulates the appetite and improves digestion. Dill marries well with salads and fish; lends aroma to meat and is mixed with other greens in herb pies. Also, it combines perfectly with cucumber, especially in the preparation of the Greek dip-appetizer known as *tzatzìki*.

Infusion: 1 cup before or during a meal to cure stomach disorders.

• Rue - "Apìganos" *(Ruta graveolens)*

Useful parts: seeds

This plant is endemic to Greece and has been cultivated since ancient times. It prefers dry and rocky ground. The rue makes a potent medicine and should be used in small quantities. It is an antispasmodic and helps cure headaches and palpitation. Also, it helps menstruation and acts as a contraceptive. It is not recommended for pregnant women.

The Chinese used it to treat snake and insect bites. Rue was a principal antidote for poisons made by the legendary Mythridàtes. If you add rue to wine, the latter does not go sour.

Infusion: 2 teaspoons of rue seeds in 1 litre of hot water cleanses the body of intestinal worms. Do not drink more than 3 cups a day every 3 or 4 hours.

• Geranium - "Abaròriza, Barbaroùssa"
(Pelargonium odoratissimum)

Useful parts: leaves

This perennial shrub originates in Africa. It has round fragrant leaves picked throughout the year for their beneficial qualities to man.

They cure peptic disorders, calm and soothe the stomach.

Owing to its aroma, the geranium leaves are used to flavour fruit pastries, particularly preserve, e.g. quince and cherries preserve.

Infusion: 1 cup soothes the peptic system.

• Basil - "Vassilikòs" *(Ocimum basilicum)*

Useful parts: leaves

It originated in India and in Greek it means royal. Basil has been in the Mediterranean for thousands of years. In southern Europe it is currently cultivated in pots that are placed outside homes and churches as its scent repels insects and flies. In addition to the sweet variety, other basil varieties differ in terms of size, shape and colour of leaves. Apart from the sweet basil other local basil varieties with various leaf sizes and colours include platìfillos (broad-leafed), sgouròs (curly), àgrios (wild), athànatos (immortal).

Basil extract has antispasmodic properties and stomach soothing properties. It is said to prevent headaches and is a tranquilliser.

In the kitchen, basil is used to season food. It is very popular in most Mediterranean cuisines. Basil is the basic ingredient in Provençal soup (France) and in Italian pesto sauce. In Crete, basil is used in red sauces and pastries.

• **Anise - "Glikànisos"** *(Pimpinella anisum)*

Useful parts: seeds

Anise seeds, sweet and aromatic, are collected by the end of summer to be used in the preparation of traditional Easter pastries (*tsourèkia*). Anise is used to add flavour to Greek and Chinese dishes.

Also, anise is used in curry powder. Star anise is used in Greek *oùzo*. Dioscurides recommended anise as a diuretic, digestive, and a herb for the treatment of headaches. Anithol and other constituents in anise's volatile oil act as insecticides, also against lice.

An anise drink is good for digestion, flatulence and colic pain. Its relaxing and expectorant action renders it useful in the treatment of coughs.

Anise drink is ideal for the treatment of intestinal complaints of babies (gas, diarrhoea, constipation).

The Japanese star anise is poisonous; it is a bush that is quite different from the four anise varieties cultivated today.

• **Laurel - "Dàfni"** *(Laurus nobilis)*

Useful parts: leaves

It is an evergreen, self-grown bush in the Mediterranean basin. Its dried leaves are used as spice in many salads. Mixed with thyme and parsley it is added to seafood, stew, lentil, chickpea and bean dishes – all cooked in the oven.

The ancient Greek physicians used a lot of laurel leaves, including the seeds, to stimulate the appetite and treat abdominal gas.

Herb tea: immerse 6-7 leaves in hot water; strain and drink before meals.

The laurel bush was dedicated to god Apollo and from its leaves the ancient Greeks made a crown for the winners in athletic events.

• **Rosemary - "Dendrolìvano"**

(Rosmarinus officinalis)

Useful parts: leaves

It is an evergreen, self-grown herb in the Mediterranean basin.

As a medicinal plant it is excellent for treating headaches, with antimicrobial and antimycotic action. This herb reduces gas and stimulates the appetite, enhancing also the functions of the bile owing to its carnosol acid, rosemaricine.

It boosts the function of the liver and improves circulation owing to its diosmin content.

Galen recommended rosemary boiled in wine for the treatment of abdominal and stomach aches. Rosemary is an ingredient of many shampoos and hair preparations. Because of its pleasant scent it is used in many beauty products. In the old days rosemary was used as incense. It adds flavour to meat, particularly lamb, and is also used in sauces that marry well with potatoes, fish, liver (savory sauce), snails, etc. As an aromatic herb it is ideal for grilled fish.

• **Dittany - "Dìktamos, Èrontas"**

(Origanum dictamnus)

Useful parts: leaves and blossomed tops

This is a low bush growing on the mountains and hills of Crete. It spreads out from its base with woolly stems. Its leaves are small and thick. Once dittany was thriving on Mount Dikti of Crete, hence its name.

It has been used since the Minoan period to ease childbirth. Because of its styptic and revitalizing qualities, people also refer to it by the name Èrontas, i.e. the herb with aphrodisiac qualities, a love potion.

Herb tea: 20-30gr in 1 - 2lt. warm water soothes migraines, neuralgia and stomach disorders.

The leaves are chewed to fight bad breath. In powder form it has antimicrobial, antimycotic, antihemorrhagic properties and helps heal wounds. Add 20-30gr of dittany powder in a glass of wine to get a tasty tonic.

- **Spearmint - "Dìosmos, Vàlsamos"** *(Mentha spicata)*

Useful parts: leaves

Dioscurides ascribed to this plant (cultivated, balsamic mint) many medicinal qualities. It helps digestion; it is also an emetic and stops hiccups. Owing to its action in the mucous of the bronchus, it stops cough, relaxes asthma and catarrh.

The spearmint is used widely in Greek cuisine: in meatballs, patties, Cretan kaltsoùnia, etc. It adds flavour to sauces, salads and soups. There is even a sauce made from spearmint.

- **Savory - "Throùbi"** *(Satureja montana)*

Useful parts: leaves

This is a perennial shrub that grows in the Mediterranean.

The carvacrol in its essential oil has potent antimicrobial properties. The ancients believed in the aphrodisiac qualities of spearmint. A decoction from spearmint has antiemetic action and fights sore throats, too.

It is used as a condiment in legumes, cabbage and red meat. It is rather bitter in taste and marries well with lima beans. Byzantine monks used spearmint to spice their soups, the agiozoùmi (àgios + zoumi = holy + broth), made from onions, olive oil and pieces of bread. Spearmint leaves are used to enhance the taste of salami/sausages.

- **Thyme - "Thimàri"** *(Thymus vulgaris)*

Useful parts: leaves, stems in bloom

It is a perennial shrub and an ideal plant for cultivating bees nearby. As a medicinal plant, it is used to treat sore throats, common colds and coughs. Thymol and carvacrol contained in its essential oils have antimicrobial and antimycotic qualities that act against tapeworms and mosquito larvae.

Use it for gargles and mouthwash. Thyme cures sore throats and inflammation of the gums. Taken as a warm infusion it is quite effective against the common cold as it increases perspiration. It is also a good expectorant; relieves one from abdominal gas and soothes the peptic system.

Thyme is used in the kitchen, with broiled meat, particularly with lamb and steaks. It adds aroma to olive oil, olives, pickles and vinegar. It also finds use in bakery and confectionery.

Extract: immerse 3 teaspoons in 1l of hot water and strain after 15 minutes.

• Cress - Kàrdamo *(Lepidium sativum)*

Useful parts: entire plant

It is an annual plant known since ancient times as an appetizer and diuretic. It is an aperient and helps the liver function. Its poultice mixed with honey is a treatment for age spots. Its flowers are excellent food sources for the bees. It contains vitamin C, iodine, iron and calcium. Cress is used also in salads.

• Coriander - "Korìandro" *(Coriandrum sativum)*

Useful parts: leaves and dried seeds

This is an annual plant originating in the East and thriving in the Mediterranean. Coriander is derived from the Greek for "bed-bug", because the smell of the fresh foliage is said to resemble that of bug-infested bed linens, which many people dislike. It is mainly used in Chinese and India cuisine. It has positive effects on the peptic system; it is used as an appetizer and its leaves are used in salads, sauces, omelettes and soups. It is also used in hare stews and lentil dishes. It adds aroma to meat, cooked pork and Greek mushroom dishes. The seeds of this plant are used in the making of curry.

Coriander seeds fight bad breath and neutralize garlic breath.

Extract: 1 teaspoon coriander seeds in 1 cup of water: boil for 15 min. Drink it after a meal to keep you awake during a trip.

• Cumin - "Kìmino" *(Cuminum cyminum)*

Useful parts: seeds

Cumin comes from Central Asia and was brought to Europe by the Arabs. Dioskourides appreciated it as it soothed the stomach and fought heartburn.

It was used by the Romans and was one of the most common seasonings in the Middle Ages. It is very widely used in Asian cuisine as well as in dishes with curry and mixtures of spices. Cumin is also used in dough used for the preparation of bread or is added to cheese, sausages and cabbage soups.

It is a basic seasoning in the famous Greek *soudzoukàkia* and it usually accompanies most pork dishes.

Extract: 1 teaspoon per cup of water. Boil for 10 minutes, filter and drink after meal.

• **Lavender - "Levànda"** *(Lavandula officinalis)*

Useful parts: dried flowers

Lavender and its oil constitute a medicine for burns and stings, heal small wounds and have powerful antimicrobic action. Lavender is ideal for the balance of the nervous system, has tranquilizing properties and is good for reducing anxiety and stress. When used in the bath it relaxes and helps, especially small children, to sleep quietly. Compresses soaked in hot herb tea from lavender blossoms soothe wounds, bruises and rheumatisms. Lavender has been used against chest infections, cough and colds as an extract. Lavender tablets protect linen from undesirable insects.

Lavender oil is very widely used in perfumery.

• **Aloysia Triphylla, Lemon Verbena - "louìza, Lemonòhorto"** *(Lippia citriodora)*

Useful parts: leaves, flower tops.

Shrub that is cultivated as an aromatic, pharmaceutical as well as ornamental plant. The leaves give off a strong lemon scent when they are rubbed.

The oil of Aloysia triphylla scents soaps and cosmetics.

Its herb tea stops diarrhoea and constitutes a

tonic with a nice aroma.

When used in cooking it flavours fish, fillings, salads, conservatives and desserts.

It is mainly used in confectionery and distilling.

• **Parsley - "Maintanòs"** *(Petroselinum crispum)*

Useful parts: leaves, root, seeds

It flourishes everywhere in the Mediterranean both in the wild as well as in cultivable form. Parsley is a powerful diuretic which fights infections of the urinary system and calculi. It is invaluable in all cases of liquid retention, oedemas, swellings in hands and legs. It is also useful against cellulite.

Being rich in vitamins (mainly A and C) and in iron, manganese, calcium and phosphorus, it is an exceptional tonic and anti-inflammatory plant. It is also beneficial against anaemia. The leaves of parsley refresh breath and constitute the traditional antidote to the unpleasant smell of garlic.

It is widely used in cooking and suits almost all recipes.

It is used in meat and fish dishes, soups, sauces, salads, omelettes, legumes, chicken dishes and, of course, as garnish and decoration.

• Greek Mountain Tea - "Malotìra, Tsài vounou" *(Sideritis syriaca)*

Useful parts: leaves, flower tops

It is a plant with thick woolly leaves and small yellow flowers. It sprouts in wild form in mountainous regions and all the mountains of Crete. Its herb tea helps digestion, colds and is a tonic and diuretic. If cinnamon and honey are added, cough is soothed.

Thanks to its flavonoid constituents it also acts against diseases of the circulatory system.

Herb tea: Two tablespoons in 1/2 litre of water. Boil for 15 minutes, until it gains colour and flavour. Serve plain or with cinnamon and honey.

• Marjoram - Matzouràna *(Origanum majorana)*

Useful parts: leaves, flower tops.

It is the cultivated variety of wild oregano. Marjoram had already been used in ancient Egypt as a spice with which priests fought migraine and nervousness.

Marjoram, which belongs to the same family as oregano, is used more as a culinary herb and less as a medicinal herb from old times until today.

It often accompanies meat, especially sausages.

Its success as a culinary herb is partly due to its digestive properties.

Infusions from this herb possess spasmolytic properties and are always recommended against migraine, the nervous tics and dysfunctions of the digestive system owing to stressful causes. Its stops stress, relaxes and contributes to a calm sleep. It gently combats blood pressure.

• Fennel - "Màratho" *(Foeniculum vulgare)*

Useful parts: seeds, tender shoots and leaves

Fennel, which is a perennial, herbaceous plant, is found in abandoned fields all over Greece. In cooking, its leaves serve as a garnish with fine and sweet flavour. It goes well with fish and other seafood, with snails, meat, sauces and legumes. Some typical Cretan dishes are: octopus with fennel, cuttlefish with fennel, without removing their ink, broad beans or beans with fennel.

The infusion of the herb or its seeds is good for colics, indigestion and heartburn.

It is also known for reinforcing the flow of milk in women who are breast-feeding.

Hippocrates and Dioscurides also recommend it.

Fennel oil is an anticonvulsant and antiibacterial.

It is an effective eyewash for tired and sore eyes. It is also a diuretic and is used for the treatment of sand and calculi of the urinary system, for liquid retention, swellings etc.
Herb tea: 2 teaspoons of seeds to a litre of water. Boil for 20 minutes and leave it for another 20 minutes before straining it.
For liquid retention: drink 1 cup 10 minutes before each meal.
For flatulence: 1 cup after each meal.

• **Lemon Balm** - **"Melissòhorto"** *(Melissa officinalis)*
Useful parts: leaves
It is an apicultural and pharmaceutical plant.
Its flower gives good quality honey to bees.
It can be found everywhere and gives off a pleasant lemon scent. It is used in cooking in order to flavour a lot of foods such as roast meat, fish, poultry and soups. Its herb tea is good for colds, flu, depression, headache and indigestion. It is served with honey.
Avicenna, an Arab doctor, recommended the plant "because it makes the heart happy." Lemon balm and its essential oil are still used in confectionery and in perfumery. The volatile oils of this plant, especially citronella, have tranquilizing properties even in minimal quantities. In the Middle Ages it constituted a basic component of the tonic liqueur "benedictin".
Its balsamic oil has antihistamine action that renders the plant suitable for the treatment of allergies such as eczema.
Key characteristics of lemon balm are its emmenagogue properties and the alleviation of menstrual pain.
Its hot extracts are perspiratory and useful for colds and flu. They have antibacterial properties and are effective against measles and labial herpes.
When prepared as an herb tea, it is preferable that it be fresh or frozen, so that its essential oils do not disappear, something that happens during the process of desiccation.
It is collected just before it blooms and is frozen or dried.

• Mint - "Mènta" *(Mentha piperita)*

Useful parts: leaves, bloomed plant.
There exist a lot of varieties of mint. The mint with long leaves and without fluff is the one used in popular medicine. It is used in cooking to enhance the flavour. The herb is an effective remedy for colic and flatulence. Menthol, the basic constituent in the volatile oil, has antibacterial and antiparasitic properties. In an alcoholic solution it is effective against lichens. Thanks to the plant colourings that it contains, it stimulates the liver and the gallbladder. Azulene contained in its oil has an anti-inflammatory and sanative effect against ulcers. Menthol can be used externally as an oil and liquid for massage. It serves as a cooling and anaesthetic agent for the skin, increasing the flow of blood where it is applied. Inhalations of mint steam have a positive result on catarrh of the upper respiratory system and the bronchi. These inhalations should be made with moderation and be avoided by children.

• Oregano - "Rìgani" *(Origanum vulgare)*

Useful parts: leaves, shoot tops
Oregano is found everywhere, mainly in the dry and warm regions of Southern Greece. It is used in all sauces that contain lemon and in Greek *horiàtiki* salad and marries well with *fèta* cheese and French fries. Dioskourides recommended it as the best medicine to those who have lost their appetite.
As an herb tea, oregano facilitates digestion and fights constipation. It is a good friend to the lungs, as it helps chronic bronchitis and also constitutes a good tonic. Because of its stimulating properties it is recommended to individuals that suffer from fatigue, exhaustion and to young girls because it promotes menstruation.

• **Celery - "Selino"** *(Apium graveolens)*

Useful parts: the whole plant

It is a biennial plant with a fleshy root. Two types are mainly cultivated. The first is cultivated for its overground part and the second type for its fleshy root.

The leaves and the sperms are rich in essential oil, fat, vasorine, mannite, organic sulphur, potassium chloride and nitric potassium and phosphorus.

Celery is suitable for diabetics, and is a diuretic. It adds a spicy flavour, which is essential in soups, fricassee, boiled meat.

It also gives flavour to all fish (gilthead sea bream with celery is a Greek dish), but it is also cooked with meat (pork with celery is a typical Greek dish).

Extract: Put 5 teaspoons of dried celery in 1 litre of water, boil for 10 minutes, let it sit for another 10 minutes and then filter. It is a precious herbal tea in slimming diets; it is a diuretic and tonic. It also cures chilblains. The seeds of celery (1 teaspoon in a cup of boiled water) or their herb tea are a diuretic and tonic.

Boiled celery in milk neutralizes uric and lactic acid, having a favourable effect on rheumatisms.

• **Rose - "Triantàfillo"** *(Rosa spp.)*

Useful parts: fruit, flowers, leaves.

Nowadays more than 20000 varieties are cultivated. They contain vitamin C, B, E, and K, nicotinamide, organic acids, tannin and pectin.

Roses are mainly used in perfumery (rose oil). Its petals and fruits are used for sweets and syrups as well as rose tea.

Rose leaves have astringent properties and are used in the healing of wounds. The extract or herbal tea of dry petals is antidiarrhetic.

The seeds were once used as a diuretic.

The rose is the flower of Venus, the ancient goddess of love, who was born in the foamy waves of Cyprus. Thus, a rose with its fine perfume grew in the coast and was seen as a welcome gift by the other gods.

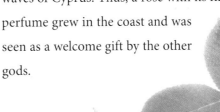

• Sage - "Faskòmilo" (Salvia officinalis)

Useful parts: leaves

The plant grows on the dry soils of the Mediterranean. Its thick, grey-white leaves contain volatile oil (cineole, borneol, linalole, thujone, salbene and camphors), plant colourings, phenolic and other acids and condensed tannins.

Its botanical name, Salvia, comes from the verb salvare that means "save". As a hot herbal tea it is good for colds. The phenolic acids that it contains are antibacterial and thujone is a powerful antiseptic. Its infusion with little vinegar makes an excellent gargle that can effectively relieve a sore throat, laryngitis and tonsillitis. As a mouthwash it is effective against gingivitis and oral ulcers. Thanks to its volatile oil, sage stimulates digestion and tones the weakened nervous system. In addition, it stops perspiration. Its estrogenic properties cure the hot flush of menopause, while it is also beneficial in cases of amenorrhoea and menstrual pain. In cooking it is used as a seasoning in poultry and meat, fish, pasta and legumes in very small quantities because of its intense flavour. Finally, it is also used as a preservative in the food and oil industry.

• Pennyroyal - "Fliskoùni" (Mentha pulegium)

Useful parts: leaves, bloomed plant.

It is a type of plant from the family of mint. Pennyroyal has been widely used from antiquity until today. It contains volatile oil up to 1% mainly pulegone, menthone etc. and tannins. It is used as an insect repellent. Its Latin name comes form the word pulex, which means "flea" thanks to its insect repellent properties. As a hot herbal tea, pennyroyal has always been a popular remedy for colds and flu, because of its sudorific properties.

In any case, it needs to be used with care, mainly during pregnancy or when expecting to become pregnant.

• Camomile - "Hamomìli"

(Matricaria chamomilla)

Useful parts: dried flowers

It is a Mediterranean, one-year-old plant that sprouts in fallow fields and at the edges of paths. Its white small flowers with the yellow centre resemble daisies, but scatter a strong distinctive smell.

Its volatile oil contains chamazulene and bisabolol that are strong antiseptics, ease pain and have inflammatory antimicrobial, anticonvulsant properties. They also heal ulcers. Belipheron has antifungal properties.

The beverage acts as a tranquilizer against insomnia, anxiety and peptic problems caused by stress. The sedative effect of chamomile is beneficial for hyper kinetic or restless children and in small quantities it is excellent for teething infants. The extract of chamomile makes a perfect lotion for cleansing the sensitive face and the buttocks of infants and gives natural bright highlights to blond hair. It is an ingredient in many cosmetics such as dyes, suntan lotions, creams etc.

Extract: Drink it hot, in a small cup, before and between meals.

In lieu of an Epilogue

Olive Tree from Vouves: Longevity and Productivity

…It had a small, thin figure when it swayed in the breath of wind and turned its little leaves to the golden sun. People collected its first fruits and Hercules Kourites* cut a branch and brought it to Olympia. The first Marathon winner was crowned with this olive branch. Later Hercules cut another branch and planted it in Olympia. A piece of it went to live in "upper" Greece.

It grew little by little…

It saw Daedalus and Icarus flying high in the sky above it. It saw huge waves covering its island. It saw people after people coming here to live. Meanwhile, a hand took care of it and it was appeased, it mellowed… And it kept growing and growing…

All sorts of people came to sit under its shade. They heard thoughts, sentiments, ideas, confessions. A Byzantine lady, a Venetian earl, a Cretan warrior, one of

Venizelos second in command, beautiful Cretan lasses and lads used to set it as a meeting point and still do.

It has grown big now. It stands as a thoughtful giant ready to give advice, to calm, to strengthen the body, the soul, the mind. Time has moulded its trunk like one of Michelangelo's sculptures – full of forms and memories. And it has survived up to this day – an imposing, distinctive and eternal presence.

The Olive Tree from Vouves, "the most Ancient Olive Tree in the World", travelled from the Cretan land to the Olympic Games, in Athens, in summer 2004. And when its branches crown the Marathon winner, the Message they will be carrying will be heard by all humanity:

"In these branches nestles the history of the Planet's Civilization."

---

* Mythical figure from Crete who first planted the olive tree in Olympia, organized races and awarded the winners with a wreath from an olive tree branch (kòtinos).

Identity:

Name:	Olive Tree from Vouves
Circumference:	12.5 metres
Diameter:	3.64 metres
Surface:	11.45 square metres
Address:	Vouves, Kolimbari, Crete
Occupation:	Diachronic Traveller, bearer of Immortality, Renewal, Peace, Reconciliation
First Trip:	Ancient Olympia
Second Trip:	Athens 2004

APPENDIX
Traditional Cretan Recipes

Soups

Kakavià soup

(serves 6)

1 1/2 cups EXTRA VIRGIN OLIVE OIL

1 kilo scorpion-fish

1/2 kilo dusky sea perch or white grouper

3 large potatoes

2 large onions

1 large lemon, juiced

Salt and pepper to taste

Spread out a layer of quartered onions in a big pot, cover with the quartered potatoes and top with the fish. Add salt and fill with water up to 4cm below the fish's surface. Then pour enough water to cover the fish.

Cover the pot and boil at high temperature for 20 minutes and then continue with the pot uncovered for another 15 minutes. Remove the soup from the heat, add lemon, cover and let stand for 10 minutes. Serve the kakavià warm with plenty of pepper.

Mushroom Soup

1 kilo fresh mushrooms

2 bunches spring onions

1 onion, small and finely chopped

1 bunch dill

1 egg

1 cup EXTRA VIRGIN OLIVE OIL

2 tablespoons dry white wine

1 lemon, juiced

Green pepper to taste

and simmer for 20 minutes.

Add the chopped spring onions and dill. Mix well and continue cooking for 15 minutes with pot covered. Add salt and/or pepper to taste. Whisk the eggs into a "foam" in a glass bowl and then gradually add small quantities of lemon juice and mushroom stock alternatingly. When done, pour the mixture from the bowl into the pot and stir well. Serve the soup warm with pepper to taste and a little fresh dill.

Clean and rinse the mushrooms under tap water. Slice them into small pieces and let them drain well. Pour and heat the olive oil in a pot, then add the onion. When the onion slices turn light brown, add the mushrooms and stir for 1-2 minutes. Then gradually pour the wine and 4 cups of water. Cover the pot

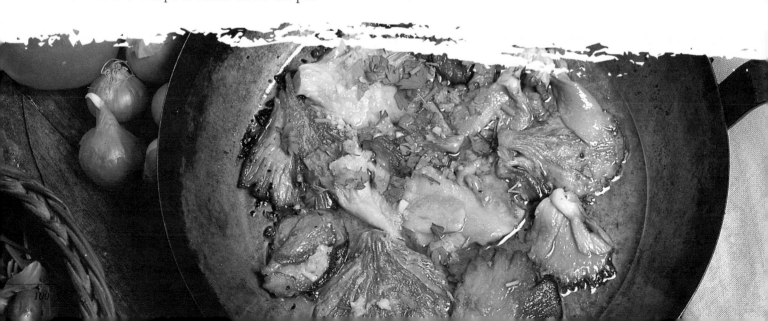

Xinòhondros soup

(Serves 4)

1/2 cup EXTRA VIRGIN OLIVE OIL

1 cup xinòhondros

5 cups water

1 tomato, medium size

Salt and pepper to taste

Pour the water, the olive oil and diced tomato in a small pot and let simmer for 4-5 minutes. Next, add the xinòhondros, season with salt and stir well. Cover the pot and continue for 35-40 minutes, but first lower the heat. Serve the soup with a lot of pepper.

Pork with hòndros soup

1 kilo pork, 1 glass hòndros

2 eggs, 2 lemons

Salt

Boil the meat. Then place it on a platter and drain off the broth. Return the broth into a clean pot, add water and when it starts boiling, add the *hòndros* and some salt. After the *hòndros* is done, remove the pot from the heat and prepare the egg-lemon sauce: first beat the two egg yolks, then add the egg whites and stir in gradually some cooking broth. Finally, place all the ingredients in the pot and stir.

Cucumber & tomato salad

(serves 4)

1 medium cucumber

3 tomatoes

5 tablespoons EXTRA VIRGIN OLIVE OIL

Salt

Oregano

Rinse the tomatoes under tap water and slice them. Then peel and chop the cucumber and place everything in a salad bowl. Season the salad with oregano and salt. Dress with olive oil.

Urchin Salad

(serves 2)

6 urchins

1 tablespoon lemon juice

3 tablespoons EXTRA VIRGIN OLIVE OIL

High-quality tsounatolado oil of incomparable flavour

A very tasty salad that can be found in most traditional fish taverns in the prefecture of Hania.

Horiàtiki salad

(serves 6)

4 tomatoes

1 cucumber

1 medium onion

1 green pepper

150gr fèta cheese

A few vinegar-cured black olives

1 bunch purslane

A little caper

1/2 cup EXTRA VIRGIN OLIVE OIL

A shot of oregano

Salt

1 teaspoon traditional vinegar

Rinse the tomatoes under tap water then peel the cucumber and slice both. Chop the onion and pepper in rounds. Put everything in a salad bowl; add the olives, caper and season with oregano, salt and mix well. Slice the *fèta* cheese and add to the salad bowl. Dress with olive oil and vinegar.

Raw spiny chicory salad

(serves 4)

200gr spiny chicory

100gr vinegar-cured black olives

2 tablespoons lemon juice

4 tablespoons EXTRA VIRGIN OLIVE OIL

Salt

Put the wild greens in a plastic bowl and top with water. Let it stand in water for about one hour. Remove the spiny chicory from the bowl and rinse well under tap water. Do not chop it. Place it back into the same or a different bowl and pour the olive oil and lemon juice over it. Season with salt, and then add black olives.

Salad with raw wild greens

(serves 4)

300gr wild greens (radish, sow thistle, fennel, arugula, salsify, leek, purslane, garden peas, etc.)

2 spring onions

1 tablespoon vinegar

4 tablespoons EXTRA VIRGIN OLIVE OIL

Salt

Rinse all the wild greens and vegetables well, then chop them. Mix them all for 1-2 minutes, then sprinkle with salt and dress with olive oil and vinegar.

Avocado salad

(serves 6)

4 avocados

4 spring onions

4 tomatoes

2 peppers

1 small cucumber

200gr fèta cheese

250gr yoghurt

4 tablespoons finely chopped dill

1 clove of garlic

Salt and pepper to taste

1 lemon, juiced

1 tablespoon EXTRA VIRGIN OLIVE OIL

Chop all vegetables and put them in a salad bowl. Prepare the sauce (dressing) with the yoghurt, garlic, pepper, dill and lemon juice and pour over the salad.

White beet and black eyed bean salad

(serves 6)

600gr black eyed beans

1 kilo white beet

1 cup EXTRA VIRGIN OLIVE OIL

2 lemons, juiced

Let the beans soften for 8 hours in cool water. Strain and transfer them to a pot with boiling water. Let them boil for 30 minutes to soften well. Rinse the white beet well and remove the hard parts and yellow leaves. Put the white beet leaves in the pot with the beans and boil for 6-7 minutes. Add lemon juice, salt and olive oil in an air-tight jar, seal the jar with its cover and shake it to mix the dressing ingredients well. Remove the jar cover and pour the dressing over the salad.

Salad with golden thistle and broad beans

(serves 4)

300gr small broad beans

1 kilo golden thistle

100gr EXTRA VIRGIN OLIVE OIL

4 tablespoons lemon juice

Salt

Place beans in a plastic bowl and top them with water. Let them stand for 8 hours to soften. Then strain and let them stand again for 25-30 minutes. Bring water to a boil in a pot and add beans. Chop the golden thistle in large pieces and boil separately for 10 minutes. Serve the broad beans and golden thistle on a platter. Whisk the lemon juice, olive oil and salt in a bowl to make the dressing and then pour over the salad.

Lima beans salad

(serves 6)

500gr lima beans

1 medium onion, finely chopped

4 tablespoons EXTRA VIRGIN OLIVE OIL

2 tablespoons lemon juice

Parsley, finely chopped

Salt

Soak the beans in cool water for 10 hours, then strain and boil for 20 minutes. Strain the beans and boil them again in fresh water for 10 more minutes. Strain and transfer them into a salad bowl. Season the beans with salt, add onions and dress them with the olive-lemon juice and top them with finely chopped parsley.

Christmas salad

(It is called Christmas salad, because the pomegranate used on Christmas day is one of the ingredients required for its preparation)

1 medium green cabbage

3 carrots, grated

2 sour apples, diced

1 cup walnuts, ground

250gr yoghurt

250gr mayonnaise

1 teaspoon mustard

The seeds from 1 pomegranate

Salt

1 lemon, juiced

Vinegar

Chop the cabbage very thinly and put it in a large salad bowl. Add the other ingredients and mix them lightly. Refrigerate the salad and serve cold. The salad should be consumed within 2 to 3 days.

Instead of mayonnaise and mustard you could use 250gr fresh cream whisked lightly.

Mixed legumes salad

(serves 6)

1 wine glass black eyed beans

1 cup small broad beans

1 cup medium size lima beans

1 cup chickpeas

1 cup wheat

1 tablespoon salt

1 cup EXTRA VIRGIN OLIVE OIL

1/2 cup lemon juice or vinegar

Soak all legumes in cool water in separate bowls and let them stand for 6 hours. First boil the wheat in a pot for 20 minutes. Replenish the water in the pot and when the wheat is done, add the broad beans, the beans and chickpeas and boil for 25 minutes. Fill the pot with fresh water and bring to a boil. Add in the salt and all legumes, including the black-eyed beans. Boil over high heat, until legumes are soft. Then strain and let them stand to drain well. Subsequently, transfer the legumes to a salad bowl and serve them warm in EXTRA VIRGIN OLIVE OIL and lemon juice or vinegar.

Dàkos – Cretan koukouvàgia

(serves 3)

3 barley rusks

6 tablespoons EXTRA VIRGIN OLIVE OIL

2 large, ripe tomatoes, peeled and grated

1 cup fèta cheese or mizìthra cheese, grated

Salt to taste

Dip the rusks half-roll slices in water to soak a little and let them stand to drain.

Next, sprinkle them with olive oil and wait, until the oil seeps into the rusk. Salt as much as you wish, according to the saltiness of the *fèta* cheese.

Top with the grated tomato and add the grated feta or *mizìthra* cheese. Serve immediately.

Dàkos with fennel and olives

3 barley rusks

10 tablespoons EXTRA VIRGIN OLIVE OIL

2 tablespoons fennel, finely chopped

1 cup cracked green olives (tsakistès), remove pits and cut flesh into small pieces

2 tablespoons fresh lemon juice

1 teaspoon lemon rind, freshly grated

Salt, coarse grain, to taste

Use a bowl to mix the cut olives, fennel, lemon rind and salt. Dip the 'Dàkos' rusks in water and then let them dry.

Pour a little olive oil over them, sprinkle them with lemon juice and top them with the mixture of olives. Serve immediately.

Pickled Bulbs

1 kilo bulbs

2 tablespoons salt, coarse grain

2 cups white wine vinegar

1 tablespoon dill, finely chopped

EXTRA VIRGIN OLIVE OIL to dress

Peel and rinse the bulbs well. Remove the root extensions. Place them in a bowl with cold water and let them soak for two days. Change the water twice a day. Use a pot to boil the bulbs for five minutes. Again, boil them in fresh water for about 10 more minutes. Transfer the bulbs to a bowl and salt them. Subsequently, transfer them into a glass jar and top them with vinegar. Seal the jar and keep it in a cool place or in the fridge. Serve the bulbs with a lot of EXTRA VIRGIN OLIVE OIL, sprinkled with chopped dill.

Salad with fennel and yoghurt

1 cup fresh fennel hearts

1 cucumber, diced

1 cup radishes, finely chopped

2 cups yoghurt, strained

1 tsp fresh mint, finely chopped

1 lemon, juiced

Salt

White pepper, freshly ground

Chop the fennels and mix with the cucumber and radishes. Add the lemon juice, season with salt and pepper and transfer the salad into a deep bowl. Add the cucumber and mint and mix all with a spatula for 2-3 minutes. Top the salad with the yoghurt and serve it garnished with the mint leaves.

Tzatzìki

Ingredients

1/2 kilo strained yoghurt

1 or 2 tablespoons EXTRA VIRGIN OLIVE OIL

2-3 tablespoons vinegar

2 large cucumbers

4-5 cloves of garlic

Salt

A little pepper

A little purslane and a little dill (optional)

Wash the cucumbers and grate them. Then, squeeze out the excess water. Peel the garlic cloves and finely chop them. Combine all the ingredients and, finally, if you wish, add the finely chopped purslane and the dill.

Skordalià

5-6 cloves of garlic

150gr potatoes (boiled)

1/2 cup EXTRA VIRGIN OLIVE OIL

2 teaspoons vinegar

Salt

Peel and mash the garlic cloves. Add in the potatoes and mash the mixture. Add 1-2 teaspoons vinegar and pour in the olive oil, whisking the mixture at the same time. Top the garlic paste with the olives and serve. In addition to olive oil, you can also add a little lemon juice. Instead of potatoes, you can use breadcrumb soaked in water.

Eggplant salad

(serves 6)

1 kilo short and round eggplants

1 cup olive oil

1 lemon, juiced

2 cloves of garlic, mashed

Salt

Prick the eggplants with a fork and cook them in the oven. When done, peel and place them in a blender along with the olive oil and salt. Blend them to a pulp, and then gradually add the garlic and olive oil in small quantities. Remove the pulp from the blender and serve in a bowl or plate.

Fish-roe salad

(serves 6)

100gr fish-roe

300gr boiled potatoes

1 cup EXTRA VIRGIN OLIVE OIL

1 small onion, grated

1 1/2 lemons, juiced

Mash the fish-roe, the potatoes and onions, until you get a smooth paste. Add the olive oil and the lemon juice in small quantities. Garnish with olives and the heart of a lettuce or with finely chopped parsley.
Instead of potatoes you can use breadcrumbs soaked in water.

Beetroot salad with yoghurt

(serves 6)

500gr yoghurt

1 kilo beetroot

4 tablespoons EXTRA VIRGIN OLIVE OIL

3 tablespoons vinegar

Salt

Clean the beetroots and bring them to a boil. Then strain and separate the roots from the sprigs and leaves.
When the roots are at room temperature, cube them. Then transfer them into a salad bowl, add all the other ingredients and mix them lightly. Transfer the salad bowl into the fridge and serve cold.
We can save the sprigs and leaves, put them in a bowl and use them as salad dressed with vinegar, olive oil and salt.

Wild amaranth with garlic

1 kilo wild amaranth

2 onions, finely chopped

4 cloves of garlic, finely chopped

2 tomatoes, finely chopped

2 potatoes, quartered

1 cup EXTRA VIRGIN OLIVE OIL

Salt and pepper to taste

Sauté the onions in olive oil and add the wild amaranth chopped. Add the potatoes, garlic, tomatoes and one cup water. Simmer for 20 minutes, then season with salt and pepper and continue simmering for 15 more minutes. Serve warm or at room temperature.

Sautéed greens

2 kilos greens (wild amaranth, nightshade)

8 small courgettes

4 potatoes

3 bunches dill, finely chopped

3 spring onions, finely chopped

2 onions, finely chopped

5 tomatoes, cut into medium-size slices

3 cups EXTRA VIRGIN OLIVE OIL

4 cups water

Salt and pepper to taste

Sauté the onions, dill and tomatoes in the olive oil for 5 minutes. Add the water, potatoes and let boil for 10 minutes. Then add the greens, courgettes, salt and pepper. Cover the pot and let them simmer for 25 minutes. Stir occasionally and add water if necessary.

Spinach rice

1 kilo spinach

2 ripe tomatoes, peeled and finely chopped

1 large onion, mashed

3 spring onions, finely chopped

1 cup parsley, finely chopped

2 cups rice

1/2 teaspoon cumin (optional)

Salt and pepper to taste

Olive oil

Remove yellow leaves from spinach and wash it well. Use a large pot to sauté the onions in olive oil. Add the spinach, tomatoes, parsley and let simmer for 12-15 minutes – do not add water.

Use a skimmer to remove the mixture and leave only a thin layer of spinach at the bottom of the pot. Apply layers alternating between rice and spinach, until all ingredients are used. Add in the spices to taste and enough water to cook the rice (normally 3 cups of water for 1 cup of rice). Next, remove the pot from the heat and cover it with a linen cloth for 10 minutes before serving.

Boiled nettles

(serves 4)

1 kilo nettles

1 wine glass EXTRA VIRGIN OLIVE OIL

1 tablespoon vinegar

Salt

Pick fresh nettles. Boil them in salted water and then strain. Pour the olive oil and vinegar over them and serve.

Bulbs with broad beans

(serves 6)

1 cup EXTRA VIRGIN OLIVE OIL

500gr dry broad beans

1 kilo bulbs

1 teaspoon oregano

Salt and pepper to taste

Peel and rinse the bulbs well. Put them in cold water for 12 hours. Do the same with the broad beans in a separate bowl. Put the bulbs in a pot with a lot of fresh water and boil them for 10 minutes. Strain and dispose of the water. Add fresh water in the pot and boil the bulbs for 15 more minutes. Place the broad beans in a pot with water and boil for 10 more minutes. Strain and add fresh water to the pot. Bring it to a boil and place the broad beans in the pot and cook for 45 minutes approximately. Taste the beans and if juicy and cooked, add in the bulbs, salt, pepper and oregano. Mix with a wooden spoon; turn heat off and let the pot stand on the stovetop for 10-15 minutes. Serve the meal in EXTRA VIRGIN OLIVE OIL.

Black-eyed beans with fennel

4 cups black-eyed beans

2 bunches fennel, finely chopped

1 large onion

3/4 cup EXTRA VIRGIN OLIVE OIL

2 fresh tomatoes, finely chopped

Salt and pepper

Boil the beans in little water for 10 minutes before cooking them. Bring water to a boil in another pot and add the beans. Let them boil for 25 minutes approximately. Strain the beans through a colander.

Use a different pot to sauté the fennel and onion a little in olive oil. Add one cup of water and let them cook for 20 minutes. Add the beans, tomatoes, salt, pepper and a little water. Let the meal simmer for 20 more minutes. Serve the meal warm or at room temperature.

Broad beans fàva

(serves 6)

600gr large broad beans

1 large onion

1 cup EXTRA VIRGIN OLIVE OIL

1 tablespoon lemon juice

Salt and pepper

Soak the broad beans in water for 9 hours. Strain and boil them in a pot with a lot of fresh water for 20 minutes. Strain and let them cool a little. Place the broad beans in another pot and top them with fresh water. Boil them for 10 more minutes. Strain again and let them cool. Remove their shells and put them in a pot along with two cups of water and salt.

Cook them, but do not cover the pot. Stir the broad beans with a wooden ladle occasionally, until they absorb their juice and turn tender. If need be, add a little water and stir, until the beans turn to puree.

Serve the puree warm in small dishes. Top each puree dish with one tablespoon of olive oil, sprinkle with a little lemon juice and finely chopped onion and pepper to taste.

Warm appetizers

Vine leaves dolmadàkia

(serves 4)

1/2 kilo vine leaves

750gr rice

2 potatoes

2 onions

2-3 courgettes

2 cups olive oil

1 lemon, juiced

Salt and pepper to taste, mint, parsley, fennel to taste

Put the vine leaves in hot water, but do not overcook, then strain and spread them out on a platter. In a bowl, place the rice and grate the courgettes, potatoes, artichokes and onions over it. Add in the finely chopped mint, cumin, salt-pepper to taste, and olive oil. Mix all ingredients very well. Pick the vine leaves one at a time and place a teaspoonful of filling from the mixture in the centre of each leaf, or spread out a little. Then fold the leaf from the long side of the filling, or in such a way as to make a secure cylinder with the leaf, so that the stuffing does not come out. Having exhausted the filling or vine leaves, spread a few vine leaves on the bottom of a large pot and carefully place the stuffed vine leaves (*Dolmàdes*). Cover the *dolmàdes* with plate (upside down), pour in hot water to top the plate and let them simmer, until they are done. When the *dolmàdes* are done, sprinkle them with lemon juice to your taste.

Lahanodolmàdes

(serves 4)

1 green cabbage (16-20 leaves required)

1/2 kilo rice

4 tomatoes

2 cups EXTRA VIRGIN OLIVE OIL

1 bunch parsley

3 onions

Mint, fennel to taste salt and pepper to taste

Cut the stem of the cabbage and then remove the leaves one by one. Bring water to a boil in a large pot and add the leaves to boil until tender, then drain and spread leaves out on a platter. Using the ingredients above, make the filling in a fashion similar to the *dolmadàkia*. Pick the leaves one at a time and slice them in half, removing the central vein. Place a teaspoonful at the tip end of each half and roll the leaf into a cylinder or from the sides (triangular fashion). Do the same with the other half of the leaf. You now have two *dolmàdes*. Pick another leaf and do the same. When you have exhausted the leaves or filling, arrange the *dolmàdes* close together in layers in a pot; top them with water and simmer for about an hour. Occasionally shake the pot by the handles, so that the *dolmàdes* do not stick to the bottom and sides of the pot.

Onion dolmàdes

(serves 4-6)

2 kilos large onions

1/2 kilo minced meat

1/2 kilo rice (rinsed)

1 ripe tomato

2 tablespoons parsley (finely chopped)

1 cup olive oil

1 teaspoon cumin

Salt and pepper to taste

Peel the onions and let them boil in a pot. When done, drain and peel off the skins to stuff them later. In the meantime you must have prepared the filling by mixing all the ingredients (minced meat, rice, tomato, parsley, half of the olive oil, cumin and salt-pepper).

Pick the onion skins one at a time and place so much filling in the centre as to secure the filling easily. Then roll or fold the skin.

Place the onion *dolmàdes* in a pot, add one cup warm water and the remaining olive oil. Cover the pot and let the *dolmàdes* simmer on moderate heat for about half an hour.

Stuffed courgette flowers

20 courgette flowers

1 cup rice

1 large tomato, grated

1 large onion, finely chopped

2 courgettes, grated

2 tablespoon parsley, finely chopped

1/2 cup olive oil for the filling

1/2 cup olive oil to cook

1/2 lemon, juiced

A dash of cumin

Salt and pepper to taste

Open the flowers to remove the pistil and all hard stems on the outside. Wash the flowers and place them in a vertical position in a bowl to drain off water entirely.

Use another bowl and place the onion, tomato, grated courgettes, parsley, rice, salt and cumin. Also, add the olive oil and mix well by hand. Pick the flowers one at a time and put in a teaspoon or less from the mixture. Fold the tips of the flowers to secure the mixture inside.

Place the stuffed flowers in a shallow and heavy-bottom baking dish. Pour 1/2 cup of olive oil, lemon juice and 1/2 cup water (maybe less) over them and simmer.

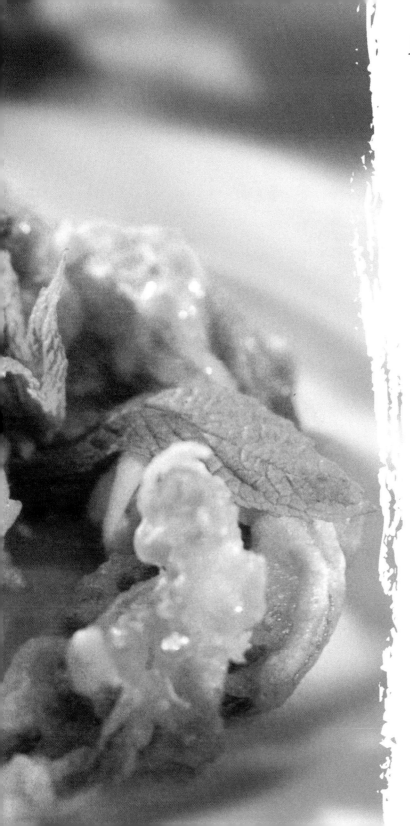

Fried sweet pumpkin

(serves 4)

1 kilo sweet pumpkin

Flour

2 cups EXTRA VIRGIN OLIVE OIL

Lemon juice or vinegar

Cut the pumpkin into long strips, 2-3cm wide. Salt pieces to taste and let them drain a little. Heat olive oil in a pan. Flour the strips and fry them over high heat. When done, remove strips onto a serving platter and sprinkle them with lemon juice or vinegar.

Meatballs

2-3 courgettes

2-3 potatoes

1 kilo minced meat

1 onion

2-3 slices stale bread, soaked in milk or wine
and strained

2-3 eggs

1 cup cheese, grated

Salt and pepper to taste

Boil the courgettes and potatoes, mash them and stir in all ingredients. Shape the meatballs, flour and fry them.

Meatballs avgolémono

1 kilo minced meat

250gr breadcrumb

2 onions

Parsley, spearmint

1 cup cheese, grated

2 egg whites

Salt and pepper to taste

Oil and flour for frying

For the sauce

2-3 onions

1 shot glass vinegar

1 wine glass milk

2 egg yolks

Prepare the mixture, shape into meatballs, dip them into flour and fry them a little. Finely chop the onions and boil them in a pot with some water. When the water is absorbed, add the butter and sauté them until slightly brown and then extinguish with vinegar. Add some more water and when it starts boiling, add the meatballs and let them boil for a while.
Beat the egg yolks, add the milk, some salt, 1 tablespoon flour, 1 tablespoon butter and several tablespoons of broth from the pot. Pour this mixture over the food in the pot, stir and turn the heat off.

Vegetable balls

4 cups EXTRA VIRGIN OLIVE OIL

1/2 sorrel, finely chopped

1/2 kilo spinach, finely chopped

1 bunch fennel, finely chopped

1 bunch dill, finely chopped

2 bunches spring onions

2 eggs

2 tablespoons rakì or oùzo

1/2 teaspoon anise, grated

1 teaspoon pepper

Salt

White all-purpose flour (as much as it takes)

Wash and rinse the vegetables well and let them drain. Chop and place all vegetables in a large bowl and season them with the salt. Use your hands to mix them well, pat them dry in your palms and place them in a new bowl. Add the eggs, pepper, anise, rakì or oùzo. Add the flour little by little, until you get a firm paste. Heat the olive oil in a deep frying pan or pot. Spoon in the mixture in amounts that correspond to a ball the size of your choice, and fry the balls until golden brown on both sides. Use a perforated skimmer to remove the balls and drain them on a paper towel.

French fries with oregano and lemon

(serves 2)

2 1/2 cups OLIVE OIL

2 large potatoes

1 teaspoon salt

1/2 lemon, juiced

oregano, grated

Peel and cut the potatoes in thick strips in a bowl. Then salt and sprinkle them with the lemon juice. Mix them well by hand. Cover and let them stand for 40-50 minutes.

Heat the olive oil in a pot or deep frying pan. Carefully transfer the potatoes into the hot olive oil and fry, until they turn golden brown. Do not cover the pot or frying pan in the process. Drain on paper towel, sprinkle with oregano and serve immediately.

French fries with stàka

(serves 2)

2 1/2 cups EXTRA VIRGIN OLIVE OIL

2 large potatoes

1 teaspoon salt

4 tablespoons stàka

Peel the potatoes and cut them in thick strips. Season them with salt and mix them well by hand. Cover and let them stand for 40-50 minutes.

Heat the olive oil in a pot or deep frying pan. Carefully transfer the potatoes into the pot or pan and fry them until golden brown. Remove the potatoes using a perforated spatula and transfer them onto a large plate. Top them with the stàka and serve immediately.

Fried eggs with tomatoes in olive oil

(serves 2)

6 tablespoons EXTRA VIRGIN OLIVE OIL

2 ripe tomatoes

4 eggs

Salt and pepper

Stàka

Heat a non-stick frying pan. Peel and grate the tomatoes, then place them in the pan. Season them with the salt and let them simmer for 6-7 minutes, until all water is absorbed. Add the olive oil, stir the mixture and simmer for 2-3 more minutes. Carefully, break the eggs over the pan; season with a little pepper and let them simmer. In the process, spoon the sauce from the pan over the eggs. When the eggs are done to your liking, remove them from the pan. Serve them with their gravy.

Sfougàto with potatoes

(serves 3)

1 cup OLIVE OIL

2 large potatoes

6 eggs

Salt and pepper to taste

Pour the olive oil in a medium size, non-stick pan and heat it well. Peel and dice the potatoes in small pieces and transfer them into the pan. Cover the pan, lower heat and cook for 20 minutes. Use a large bowl to whisk the eggs and season them with salt. Drain the potatoes on a paper towel and place them in the bowl with the eggs. Mix well. Transfer the mixture of eggs and potatoes into a lightly oiled pan and let the omelette cook on one side for 7-8 minutes over low heat. Turn the omelette over and cook for 7-8 minutes more. Turn it two more times and when done, serve warm or cold and season with a little pepper.

Eggs with stàka

(serves 2)

4 eggs

4 tablespoons stàka

Salt

Add water and salt in a frying pan and bring to a boil. Break the eggs in the boiling water; spoon boiling water over them, until the eggs turn into 4 white balls. Remove the eggs from the pan and serve each with two tablespoons of *stàka*.

Stewed okras with potatoes

(serves 6)

1 cup EXTRA VIRGIN OLIVE OIL
1 kilo fresh okras
2 large potatoes
1 large onion
2 large, ripe tomatoes
2 tablespoons parsley, chopped
1 lemon, juiced
Salt and pepper

Clean the okras and rinse them well, then strain and season them with salt. Pour the olive oil in a pot and heat it slightly over low heat. Add the onion chopped in thin slices and sauté for 2-3 minutes, but don't let it get golden brown. Add the potatoes and two cups of water. Cover the pot and simmer for 20-25 minutes.

Then add the parsley, okras, tomatoes (diced into small pieces) and a cup of water. Cover the pot and simmer for approx. 15 minutes. Uncover the pot, raise heat and continue cooking for 20 more minutes.

Five minutes before this time expires, add the lemon juice, salt, pepper. Then raise and shake slightly by holding the handles. Do not use a fork to stir. Replace the pot on the stovetop, turn heat off, and let pot stand over heat for 6-8 more minutes. Serve warm or cold.

Artichokes with broad beans

(serves 6)

1 kilo artichokes

1 kilo broad beans

1 cup EXTRA VIRGIN OLIVE OIL

2 fresh garlic heads

1 bunch dill

2 tablespoons flour

2-3 tablespoons vinegar

Salt

Place olive oil and two glasses of water in a pot and boil the green beans for 15 minutes. Then add the artichokes, garlic heads, the finely chopped dill and the salt. When the ingredients are almost done, place flour in a bowl and dissolve with a little water. During this process add vinegar little by little and do the same with some juice from the meal in the pot. When you get a thick paste in the bowl, add it to the pot, stir a little and let boil for a couple of minutes. Then turn the heat off.

Stewed mushrooms with chestnuts

(serves 4)

1 1/2 kilos mushrooms

1/2 kilo onions

1/2 water glass EXTRA VIRGIN OLIVE OIL

2 medium size tomatoes

3/4 kilo chestnuts

Salt and pepper

Clean and rinse the mushrooms well. Heat the olive oil in a pot; add in the mushrooms and the onions chopped coarsely, salt and pepper to taste and sauté. Next, add the grated tomatoes. Ten minutes before you take the pot off the stovetop, add the chestnuts that you have previously boiled or braised for approximately 20 minutes.

Sweet pumpkin with chestnuts and olives

(serves 6)

2 kilos sweet pumpkin

1 cup EXTRA VIRGIN OLIVE OIL

3 bay leaves

a few spring onions

2 cloves of garlic

1 red hot pepper

1 cup xinòhondros

2 cups chestnuts

1 cup green olives

Salt

Cut the pumpkin in medium size pieces. Cut the onions, pepper and chestnuts in smaller pieces. Pour the olive oil in a pot and add all the ingredients. Stir to mix. On first boil lower the temperature to moderate heat, so that the ingredients cook in their juice. Do not add water.

Giant Beans (Gìgantes) in the oven

(serves 6)

1 cup EXTRA VIRGIN OLIVE OIL

500gr giant beans (gìgantes)

2 onions

1 bunch parsley

2 cloves of garlic

1 teaspoon tomato paste

1 ripe, large tomato

1 medium size tomato

1 teaspoon oregano

1/2 teaspoon cumin

3-4 drops lemon juice

1 teaspoon sugar

Salt and pepper

Let the beans soak in water for 8 hours. Boil them in a pot for 25 minutes; strain and rinse them under tap water. Finely chop the onion, garlic and sauté them in olive oil. Add the finely chopped celery, tomato paste (dissolved in water), spices, sugar and lemon juice. Stir and add 1 cup of water. Boil the sauce for 20 minutes approximately.

Place the giant beans in a baking pan and pour the sauce over them. Garnish the beans with the tomato slices; season with a little salt and pepper and bake for 30-40 minutes at 180°C.

Serve warm or at room temperature.

Stewed eggplants with fèta cheese

(serves 6)

1 kilo eggplants

1 large onion

1 1/2 large tomatoes

1/2 tablespoon tomato paste

1 tablespoon parsley, chopped

300gr hard fèta cheese

1 cup EXTRA VIRGIN OLIVE OIL

Salt and pepper

Clean, wash and cut the eggplants in small pieces. Pour the olive oil in a pot and heat it slightly. Add the coarsly chopped onion, stir and sauté for 1-2 minutes.

Then add the chopped eggplant and 1 cup of water. Cover the pot and simmer for 10 minutes approximately. Dissolve the tomato paste in a cup of water and add it to the pot, along with the fresh, diced tomato and parsley. Season with salt and pepper; stir with a perforated skimmer and cover the pot to simmer for 40-45 minutes.

Uncover the pot, raise it a little and shake it slightly. Do not stir using a fork. Continue cooking with the pot uncovered for 10-12 more minutes.

When the eggplants are done (only their juice and olive oil remain in the pot), add the *féta* cheese and cover the pot. Turn the heat off and let the pot stand on the hot ring for 15 more minutes, until the *féta* cheese melts. Serve warm or at room temperature.

Stuffed eggplants

(serves 4)

6 small eggplants

3 cloves of garlic, finely chopped

1 onion, finely chopped

3 tablespoons mint, finely chopped

3 tablespoons parsley, finely chopped

1/2 tablespoon salt

2 pinches of red pepper

150gr mizìthra cheese

50gr ladotìri cheese

50gr gravièra cheese

4 tomatoes

Preferably grill eggplant or bake in the oven at a high temperature. Scoop out, but set aside, the pulp from the eggplants. Keep the eggplant hulls nearby for stuffing later. In a pot, lightly sauté the garlic and onion over low heat. Add in the mint and parsley; stir to mix. Use a bowl to mix the ingredients in the pot with the eggplant pulp, adding also the grated cheese (*ladotìri* and *gravièra* cheese). Stuff the eggplants with the filling and place them in a baking pan. Pour the grated tomatoes over the eggplants. Sprinkle with salt and pepper to taste, add olive oil and cook in the oven at a moderate temperature for 20 minutes.

Eggplants with rice

(serves 6)

1 kilo eggplants
1 cup olive oil
1 onion
3 tomatoes
2 cups rice
5 glasses water
Salt and pepper

Sauté the onion in olive oil and add the chopped eggplants. Add the ground tomatoes, let them boil for a while and add water, salt and pepper. Then pour the rice and let boil until done.

Eggplants stew

1 kilo long eggplants
3-4 onions
1 cup olive oil
1/2 kilo tomatoes
Salt and pepper to taste
1 small cup vinegar

Pour the olive oil in a pot; add the onions and sauté lightly. Add the eggplants and sauté for 10 minutes approximately. In the meantime, peel and chop the tomatoes in small pieces. Add the tomatoes into the pot, salt and pepper to taste and let all cook. When the eggplants are almost done and before you take the pot off the ring, pour in the vinegar.

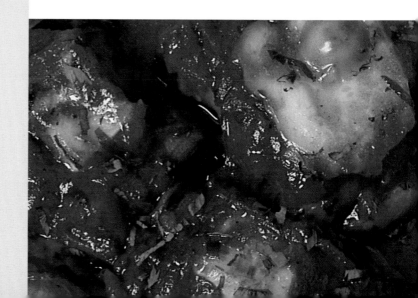

Stuffed courgettes

(serves 4)

10 medium size courgettes

1/2 kilo mizithra cheese

5 tablespoons fennel, finely chopped

5 spring onions

Salt to taste

Coarsely ground pepper to taste

6 tablespoons stàka

Boil the courgettes for 10 minutes until crispy. Mix the *mizìthra* with the fennel and onions for the filling. Slice the courgettes lengthwise to remove pulp and seeds and sprinkle with salt and pepper. Stuff the courgettes with the filling and place them in a baking pan. Add the *stàka* and bake for 15 minutes, until the courgettes are golden brown.

Courgettes with garlic in the oven

(serves 6)

2 kilos courgettes

7-8 cloves of garlic, finely chopped

4 tomatoes

Parsley

1 cup EXTRA VIRGIN OLIVE OIL

Salt and pepper

Wash the courgettes and carve them across with a knife to tuck in the garlic. Place the courgettes neatly into a baking pan. Add in the olive oil and the grated tomatoes; sprinkle with the dill, salt and pepper to taste, and cook in the oven for an hour. Sprinkle with parsley again.

Gemistà

5-6 large tomatoes

2-3 eggplants

2-3 courgettes

2-3 peppers

2-3 potatoes

2 onions

Dill, parsley

1 cup olive oil

1/2 kilo rice

1 1/2 cups fresh cream or grated cheese

Hollow out the tomatoes, eggplants and courgettes and place their pulp in a bowl. Finely chop and add to the pulp the rice, salt, pepper, olive oil and finely chopped onion, dill and parsley and mix. Season the scooped tomatoes, courgettes, eggplants and peppers and stuff each with the mixture.

Place the stuffed vegetables in a baking pan and top them with a tablespoon of fresh cream or just before you turn off the oven sprinkle them with a little grated cheese.

Stuffed tomatoes with rice and fennel

6 large, ripe tomatoes

8 tablespoons glazed rice

4 large onions, finely chopped

1 large bunch fennel

2 carrots, grated

1 artichoke, grated

2 courgettes, grated

1 cup olive oil

1 teaspoon sugar

A shot of oregano

Salt and pepper

7 large vine leaves

Olive oil to cook in

Cut off the top of tomatoes, but save tops for later use, and scoop out the pulp from the inside of tomatoes – leave skin only, but save the pulp also. Season the inside of tomatoes with salt to taste and place them upside-down on a dish to drain.

In a large bowl, mix in olive oil, tomato pulp (mashed), onions, carrots, artichoke, courgettes, fennel, rice, oregano, sugar and salt-pepper. Stir the ingredients well by hand. Stuff the tomatoes with the filling and cover them with the tops you saved earlier. Place the tomatoes in a baking pan and cover them with vine leaves, so that they do not get burnt in the process. Over the vine leaves grate a large tomato, pour with the olive oil and place the pan in the oven. Cook at 150°C for an hour and a half. Fifteen minutes earlier, remove the burnt vine leaves and let the tomatoes cook a little. Serve the meal slightly warm or at room temperature.

Baked spinach pie

(serves 6)

For the dough:

1 cup EXTRA VIRGIN OLIVE OIL

2 eggs

1 teaspoon salt

11/2 cup milk

700gr soft white flour

1 cup sesame for sprinkling

1 egg yolk to spread on top

For the filling:

3 tablespoons EXTRA VIRGIN OLIVE OIL

1 kilo spinach

1 bunch parsley

8 spring onions, only the green part

2 tablespoons spearmint, finely chopped

2 cups sour mizithra cheese

Salt and pepper

Place the eggs, olive oil, milk, salt and two cups of flour in a bowl. Work the mixture by gradually adding the equivalent amount of flour and knead into a dough. Check its density by hand and knead on a floured surface for 4-5 minutes. Cover with a linen cloth and let it rest, until you prepare the stuffing.

Combine the finely chopped spinach and parsley in a big bowl. Dip your hands in plenty of salt and rub the spinach and parsley, until they shrivel up and acquire a vivid, deep green colour. Mix them with the finely chopped onions, spearmint, pepper and sour *mizithra* cheese.

Divide the dough in half. Mix the finely chopped spinach and parsley in a big bowl. Slightly oil a round baking pan and lay the pastry sheet, so that an overhang is created. Empty the filling onto the pastry sheet and spread it uniformly with a spoon. Cover with a second pastry sheet and fold it around attaching the one with the other.

Brush the pie with the beaten yolk. Sprinkle sesame over it and bake for 40-45 minutes at 180°C. Let the pie cool before cutting. It can also be eaten cold

Small spinach pies with spearmint

Ingredients for the dough

2 eggs

1 cup milk

1 cup olive oil

700gr soft white flour

1 teaspoon salt

Ingredients for the filling

1 kilo spinach

1 bunch parsley

6-8 spring onions (only the green part)

2 tablespoons spearmint, finely chopped

2 cups sour mizìthra cheese

Salt and pepper to taste

Egg yolk

Sesame

Put the eggs, olive oil, milk, salt and 2 cups flour in the blender and beat them all gradually adding the flour to form a soft dough. Let stand for about 20 minutes. Meanwhile, wash and finely chop the spinach and parsley, rub and salt them. Mix with the spring onions, spearmint, pepper and sour *mizìthra* cheese.

Divide the dough in half and roll out small round circles, approximately 7-8cm in diameter each. Place filling in the centre of the circle and seal the edges pressing with a fork. Spread the pies with the beaten yolk, sprinkle sesame over them and bake in 180°C for 20 minutes, until their surface becomes slightly brown.

Onion pie

(serves 6)

Ingredients for the filling

1 kilo spring onions or onions

5 eggs

2 cups olive oil

Salt and pepper to taste

1 cup cheese

Ingredients for the dough

1 cup water

1 cup olive oil

1 egg

Some salt, some yeast

1/2 kilo flour

Dissolve yeast in hot water, add olive oil, egg, salt and flour and work into a dough. Leave the dough covered to rise.

Chop the onions and sauté them. Afterwards, add the eggs, cheese, salt and pepper.

Roll out 2 thick pastry sheets. Lay out the first on an oiled baking pan, evenly distribute the filling on top and cover with the second one. Brush with oil and bake the pie at a moderate temperature until brown.

Leek pie

Ingredients for the dough

1 kilo hard flour

1 cup olive oil

1 teaspoon fresh yeast

1 teaspoon salt

Tepid water

1/2 cup olive oil

Ingredients for the filling

1 1/2 kilos leeks

350gr fèta cheese

3 eggs

150gr olive oil

1 tablespoon salt

1 teaspoon pepper, freshly ground

Place the olive oil, yeast (dissolved in 1 cup tepid water), salt and flour into a bowl and work the mixture gradually adding some tepid water. Knead into a smooth and soft dough. Allow it to stand for about 20 minutes and prepare the stuffing. Finely chop the leeks, salt them and rub them in order to obtain a deep green mass. After straining the liquids well mix them with the *fèta* cheese, beaten eggs, olive oil and pepper.

Roll out 7 pastry sheets and brush both sides with oil. Spread out 3 of them on an oiled baking pan. Lay the 1/3 of the filling and cover with a new pastry sheet. Continue successively and top with two oiled leaves. Fold the part of the pastry sheets that is overhanging, score the pie, oil its surface and bake in preheated oven at 170°C for about 60 minutes.

Wild amaranth pie

(serves 4)

Ingredients for the filling

1 kilo wild amaranth

2 cloves of garlic

Spring onions

2 bunches parsley

Salt and pepper to taste

4 tablespoons olive oil

Ingredients for the dough

1/2 kilo flour

1 cup olive oil

1 cup water

1 egg

Some salt, some yeast

Cut the silver beets and sauté them with plenty of finely chopped onion, parsley, garlic, salt and pepper. Then, cook and strain. Proceed with the preparation of the dough and roll out 2 thick pastry sheets. Lay the first on the baking pan and spread out the wild amaranth on top. Cover with the second sheet, brush the pie with olive oil or butter and bake at moderate temperature until brown.

Nettle pie

(serves 6)

Ingredients for the filling

1 kilo nettles

2 large onions, finely chopped

3 spring onions, finely chopped

4 teaspoons olive oil

Salt

Ingredients for the dough

1/2 kilo flour approx.

1 cup olive oil

1/2 tablespoon salt

3 tablespoons vinegar

1 tablespoon fresh yeast

11/2 cup sesame

Some yellow cheese

Boil the nettles and combine with the remaining ingredients for the stuffing. Slightly sauté the onions beforehand. Use the ingredients for the dough to make 2 pastry sheets as follows: mix the salt with the flour and add the oil, vinegar and yeast dissolved in 1 cup of tepid water. Work the materials well, adding a little tepid water, until the dough is homogeneous and smooth. Let it stand for about 20 minutes and halve it.

Then roll out 2 pastry sheets of 4-5mm thickness each. Lay the first on a greased baking pan, place filling on it and cover with the second pastry sheet. Brush the pie with egg or olive oil and sprinkle with plenty of sesame seeds. Bake at moderate temperature for about 50 – 60 minutes.

Bourèki from Hania

Ingredients for the dough

1/2 kilo flour

3 teaspoons olive oil

1/2 teaspoon salt

1 glass red wine

1 glass tepid water

Ingredients for the filling

1 1/2 kilos potatoes, cut into thin rounds

1 1/2 kilos courgettes, cut into thin rounds

1 bunch spearmint

1 glass flour

1 kilo mizìthra cheese

200gr kassèri cheese, grated

1 cup olive oil

1 glass milk

2 eggs

4 tablespoons stàka

Sesame seeds for sprinkling

Salt and pepper to taste

First, prepare the pastry dough by combining water, olive oil, salt and wine with the flour and kneading well. Allow to rest for 30 minutes. Divide the dough in half and roll out two moderate pastry sheets. Lay one pastry sheet on a large greased baking pan.

Layer the potatoes, courgettes and *mizìthra* cheese. Sprinkle each layer with a little salt, pepper, spearmint, flour and the grated *kassèri* cheese. Whisk the eggs with milk and *stàka* and pour this mixture on top. Pour with olive oil. Top with the other pastry sheet, brush it with a little oil and sprinkle sesame on top. Cut the patty in square pieces and bake for 11-15 minutes at 180°C.

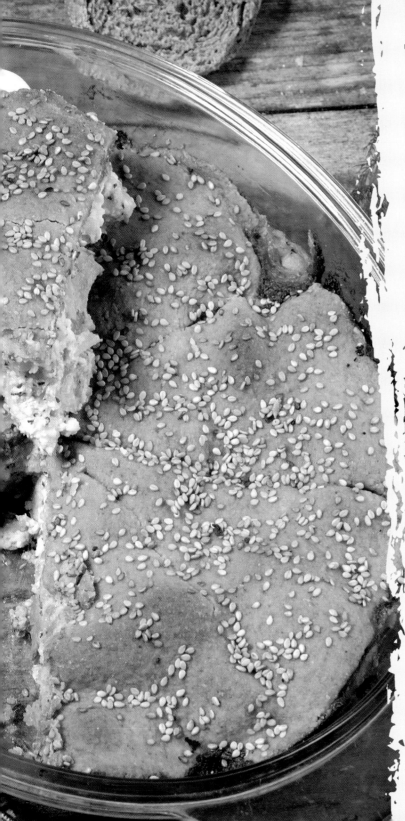

Sweet pumpkin pie

Ingredients

For the filling

1 1/2 kilos pumpkins

2 onions

1/2 kilo féta cheese

2-3 eggs

For the dough

1 cup olive oil

Flour, as required

2 eggs

Salt

1 cup milk

1 teaspoon baking powder

Sauté the pumpkin with the onion and cook, until it becomes mushy. Strain and add the spearmint, grated *fèta* cheese and eggs. Use the ingredients for the dough to prepare two pastry sheets. Spread out the first on an oiled baking pan, lay the filling on top, cover with the second pastry sheet and bake in the oven until brown.

Small vegetable pies

(serves 4)

1 kilo spinach

1 bunch parsley

1/2 cup spearmint, finely chopped

1/2 cup fennel or dill, finely chopped

1 wine glass EXTRA VIRGIN OLIVE OIL

Some spring onions

1 cup onions, chopped or grated

1 bunch wild aromatic greens

1/2 kilo mizìthra cheese (optional)

Salt and pepper

Wash greens and let them strain well. Finely chop and salt them rubbing them, until they shrivel. Then, add the parsley, spearmint, as well as the spring onions, oil, pepper, *mizìthra* cheese and mix well. Roll out a pastry sheet, not a very thin one, cut into rounds using a saucer, place the filling, fold over and press the edges with the tines of a fork to seal in the filling. Brush them with egg, if you wish, top with a little sesame and bake at 180-200°C for about half an hour.

Small pumpkin pies

Ingredients

For the filling

2 kilos sweet pumpkins

3-4 eggs

1 cup olive oil

2 onions

2 cups cheese, grated

Spearmint, salt, pepper, cumin

For the dough

1 kilo flour

2 glasses water

2 teaspoons salt

1 cup olive oil

1 teaspoon vinegar

Chop the pumpkin and sauté with finely chopped onion in olive oil. Stir continuously, until a fine purée is achieved and its liquid is absorbed. Strain the pumpkin, combine with the eggs, cheese, spearmint if you prefer. Season with salt, pepper and enough cumin. Knead the dough, roll out a pastry sheet and use a saucer to cut the dough into circles. Spoon 1/2 tablespoon of filling onto each piece and seal well. Fry in hot olive oil.

Fried small vegetable pies

Ingredients for the filling

1/2 kilo spinach

1 bunch fennel

5 spring onions, finely chopped

2 tablespoons leek (only the green part)

finely chopped

1 teaspoon salt

1 teaspoon pepper

Ingredients for the dough

500gr white flour

3 teaspoons olive oil

1 tablespoon lemon juice

1 cup tepid water

Very little salt

Olive oil for frying

Wash very well, strain and finely chop the spinach and fennel. Sauté spring onions in olive oil for 3-4 minutes. Add the spinach, fennel and two cups of water and simmer for about 45 minutes. After liquid is absorbed, season with salt and pepper and, when the greens cool, pour them into a colander, so that the oil is strained.

Prepare the dough for the pastry sheet and leave it aside for 20 minutes. Then roll out the pastry sheet and cut circles of 8cm each. Place a small quantity of greens on each circle, carefully fold them into small crescents and seal them by pressing the edges with the tines of a clean fork.

Fry the small vegetable pies in abundant hot oil on both sides until well browned. Serve them slightly warm or at room temperature.

Fish pie

(serves 4)

For the filling

200gr tuna

500gr boiled potatoes

2 onions, finely chopped

For the dough

1 cup olive oil

salt, water

1/2 kilo flour

To prepare the filling, mix the tuna with potatoes and onion and season with salt and pepper. Then prepare the dough and roll out two pastry sheets. Layer the first one on the baking pan, spread the stuffing on top and cover with the second pastry sheet. Brush the top pastry sheet with oil or egg and bake the pie, until its surface turns brown.

Chicken pie with mushrooms

Ingredients

1 medium sized chicken

500gr mushrooms

250gr ham

250gr cheese, various types

1 cup chicken stock

1 tablespoon corn flour

2 egg whites

Parsley

2-3 cloves of garlic

4 sheets phyllo pastry or 2 homemade pastry sheets

150gr olive oil

Boil the chicken, remove the bones and chop it in bite-sized pieces. Sauté with oil, add the mushrooms, garlic, ham and parsley. Layer two phyllo-sheets or one homemade one on an oiled baking pan and place the filling and cheese on top. Combine a cup of meat stock, one tablespoon corn flour and two egg whites and prepare a cream. Pour over the filling. Top with the other two phyllo-sheets (or one homemade one), brush with a little evaporated milk and sprinkle with sesame. Bake the pie at a moderate temperature for about half an hour.

Meat pie from Hania

Ingredients

For the dough

1/2 kilo flour

1 small carton yoghurt

1/2 cup oil

Some salt

1 cup meat stock

For the filling

1 kilo lamb or kid

1 kilo mizìthra cheese

1 glass stàka

Pepper, cinnamon, spearmint

1 cup meat stock

1 tablespoon corn flour

After boiling the meat and removing its bones, chop it and sprinkle with salt, pepper, spearmint and cinnamon. Prepare the dough by first combining the flour with oil and then add the rest of the ingredients for the dough. When the dough is done, spread out half of it on an oiled baking pan. Spread out half of the *stàka*, *mizìthra* cheese and the all the meat. Top the meat with the remainder of the *mizìthra* cheese and *stàka* and sprinkle again with cinnamon and spearmint. Roll out another pastry sheet and cover the pie. Brush with the beaten egg, sprinkle with sesame seeds and bake for 1 hour at a low temperature. Follow the same procedure to prepare individual pies.

Crêpes

Ingredients for the crêpes

1 cup flour
1 cup olive oil
1 teaspoon salt
4 eggs, beaten
2 cups milk

Ingredients for the filling

1/2 kilo minced meat
1/2 cup oil or butter
2 spring onions or 1 onion
3 eggs
1 cup cheese, grated
Salt, pepper and some nutmeg

Beat all ingredients into a thin batter. Brush the frying pan with oil and put 1/2 small cup of the already prepared batter. Shake it to cover the entire surface of the frying pan and place over the heat to thicken. Then remove from the heat and carefully turn it over with a wooden spatula and let it cook on the other side. Fry all crêpes in the same way and let them cool.

Sauté minced meat with oil and onions (without any tomato), place it in a bowl and add the egg, cheese, pepper and salt.

In a small pan, prepare a thick cream with 2 tablespoons of butter (heated until hot), 2 tablespoons of flour, 1 cup of milk, one beaten egg and some nutmeg. Beat two eggs, dip the crêpes in and then roll them in breadcrumb. Fry over moderate heat.

If you wish, sprinkle them with cheese and after oiling a baking pan bake them in the oven for half an hour. Sprinkle with tomato before transferring to oven.

Spread the cream and minced meat over the crepes and roll them up.

Kalitsoùnia from Hania

Ingredients

For the dough

1 kilo flour

1 teaspoon salt

1 cup olive oil

1 glass milk

2 eggs

Some coriander, pounded

Some mastic, pounded

For the filling

2 kilos mizìthra cheese

3-4 eggs

3 tablespoons spearmint, finely chopped

Prepare the dough and let it rest for approximately 1 hour. Beat the olive oil and 1/2 glass of water and combine them all with the yeast. Mix well and add the milk and eggs. Continue kneading by gradually pouring the remainder of the flour and the rest of the ingredients for the dough. Knead the dough well and leave it aside. Mix well all ingredients for the filling. Then roll out a pastry sheet and cut circles in the size of a saucer. Place a tablespoonful of *mizìthra* cheese on each circle and fold into squares. Brush with egg, sprinkle with sesame seeds and bake in the oven.

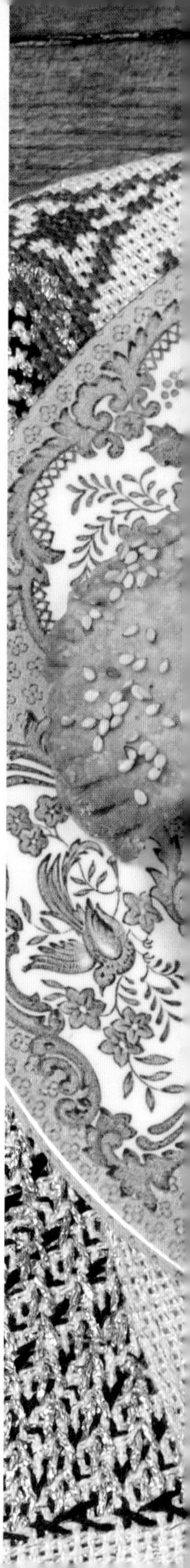

Kalitsoùnia

(20-30 servings)

2 kilos spinach or other greens

1/2 cup olive oil

Salt, pepper, spearmint

1 onion

Wash spinach well and chop. Put in an empty pot and cook for 5 minutes, until it shrivels, squeeze it dry with your hands and transfer it into a bowl. Add the finely chopped onion, salt, pepper, spearmint, olive oil and mix. Roll out a pastry sheet in the size of a saucer. Fill each leaf with one tablespoon of the prepared filling, fold it, seal well and fry in hot oil on both sides, or bake in the oven at 180°C. If you bake the *kalitsoùnia* in the oven, brush them with beaten yolk and sprinkle with sesame seeds beforehand.

Fried kalitsoùnia with onion

Ingredients for the filling

2 cups olive oil

5 cups spring onions

1 large onion

2 cups spinach

2 tablespoons spearmint

2 tablespoons dill

2 cups sour mizìthra cheese

1 teaspoon salt

1 tablespoon pepper

Ingredients for the dough

3 cups all purpose flour

2 tablespoons lemon juice

3 tablespoons EXTRA VIRGIN OLIVE OIL

3 cups olive oil for frying

1 teaspoon salt

Tepid water for kneading

Combine the spinach, spring onions, spearmint and dill, all finely chopped, in a bowl. Sprinkle with salt and work the greens by hand pressing water out, until they shrivel. Drain the water off and place in a clean bowl. Season with pepper, add the olive oil, sour mizìthra cheese and finely chopped onion to the mixture. Mix all the ingredients by hand to obtain a uniform mixture. Cover, allow to stand in the refrigerator, until you have prepared the dough.

In a clean bowl place the flour, make a hole in the middle and fill with olive oil, salt and lemon juice. Gradually add some tepid water and continue working by hand into a somewhat soft dough.

Allow to stand for 10 minutes. Then divide it into pieces and roll them out into fine pastry sheets. Cut small circles on each sheet and place a teaspoon of filling in the centre of each one. Shape into crescents and press the edges with the tines of a fork so as to seal the small pastry envelopes.

Heat olive oil and transfer the onion pies one by one into it. Fry them until slightly brown. Remove with a perforated skimmer and place them on a paper towel to drain off the oil. Serve hot or cold.

Fried Kalitsoùnia from Hania

(40 servings)

Ingredients

For the dough

2 kilos flour

2 teaspoons salt

1/2 EXTRA VIRGIN OLIVE OIL

1 cup tsikoudià

3 glasses water

For the filling

1/2 kilo mizìthra cheese

1/2 kilo anthòtiro cheese

1/2 kilo malàka cheese

3 eggs

Prepare the dough with the flour, olive oil, *tsikoudià*, water and salt. Combine with the *anthòtiro, mizìthra, malàka* cheese as well as the eggs. Roll out a pastry sheet and cut circles in the size of a saucer. Spoon some filling on each piece, fold, and seal edges by pressing very well and then fry in plenty of oil.

Snails boubouristì

1 kilo snails

1 wine glass red wine or vinegar

1 wine glass flour

1 cup olive oil

Salt, pepper, rosemary

Place the snails in a container with water and let them stand. When they project their heads from the shell (1/2 and 3/4 of an hour), rinse them thoroughly. Discard the snails that have not projected their heads from their shells. Fill half the pot with water and bring to a boil. Then, pour the snails in and add 3 tablespoons salt. When foam begins to rise to the surface, add a wine glass of vinegar and let them boil for 10 minutes. Afterwards drain water and leach out thoroughly with cold water.

Salt snails, flour them, place them in a frying pan with hot olive oil with the orifice facing downwards and fry for 3 minutes. Season with rosemary, salt, pepper. Stir once and extinguish with wine after 2 minutes. Let them boil and when done, serve.

Potatoes with snails and fennel

1/2 kilo snails

1 large bunch fennel

4 potatoes, quartered

1 large onion, finely chopped

2 ripe tomatoes, finely chopped

3 tablespoons red wine

3/4 cup olive oil

Salt and pepper to taste

Place the snails in a deep bowl filled with tepid water and cover with a dish. Allow them to stand for 30 minutes. When the snails begin to move, remove the thick membrane covering their orifice with a knife and scrub any other waste from their shell (if a snail has not come off its shell, it is probably not alive). Rinse meticulously under plenty of tap water and let them boil in some saltwater for 5 minutes. Take them out with a ladle, put them into a colander and pour off any excess liquid. Sauté the onion with the olive oil in a saucepan, add the fennel, stir and extinguish with wine. Add 1 cup of water and let food simmer for about 25 minutes. Then add the potatoes, snails, tomatoes, salt and pepper. Continue boiling for 30 minutes over moderate heat. Serve slightly warm or at room temperature.

Snails with potatoes and courgettes

(serves 6)

1 kilo snails

6 medium-sized potatoes

5 courgettes

3 medium-sized ripe tomatoes

2/3 glass olive oil

1 medium onion

Salt and pepper to taste

1 bunch parsley

2 cloves of garlic

Heat the oil in a skillet and add the snails, ground tomato, parsley, garlic and chopped onion. Season with salt, pepper and sauté for 2-3 minutes. Next, add the chopped potatoes and the whole courgettes and let them boil over moderate heat for about 20 minutes. Add some more water during the process, if required.

Snails in tomato sauce with French fries

(serves 6)

1 kilo snails

1 kilo potatoes

1 onion

1/2 kilo tomatoes

Olive oil, salt, pepper

Sauté the onion in olive oil. Finely chop the tomatoes and add them in the pot. Then add water and bring to a boil. Add the snails in the pot. At the same time, slice the potatoes and fry them. Add the potatoes in the pot, when the snails start boiling. Season with salt and pepper and let them boil.

Stewed Snails

(serves 4)

1 kilo snails

1 cup virgin olive oil

1 tablespoon flour

2 lemons, juiced

Prepare the snails in the same manner described above.

Instead of small snails, which is usually the case, you can opt for larger ones, if you wish. Place the snails again in an empty pot, pour olive oil, lemon and 1/2 teaspoon flour over them and let them boil. Serve straight away.

Fried snails

(serves 4)

1 kilo large snails

2 cups olive oil for frying

Salt, vinegar

Prepare the snails as mentioned above.
Leach them out thoroughly under tap water and then put them in a frying pan with their shells facing upwards.
Fry over high heat while stirring occasionally.
Just before they are done add salt and vinegar and serve.

Snails with eggplants

(serves 6)

1 kilo snails

2 cups EXTRA VIRGIN OLIVE OIL

1 onion

1 kilo eggplants

1 glass trahanàs

1/2 kilo ripe tomatoes

Salt and pepper to taste

Chop the eggplants, salt them and allow to stand for about 1 hour. Rinse and strain them. Afterwards, sauté them in olive oil and onion and add the snails, the grated tomatoes and let them boil for a while.

Pour 2-3 more glasses of water, bring them to a boil and add *trahanàs*, salt and pepper. Continue boiling, until thoroughly cooked.

Snails with vine shoots and wild carrot

1/2 kilo snails

1 bunch vine shoots

1 bunch tender wild carrot tops

Olive oil

Vinegar

Salt

Clean and leach out the snails very well and remove the membranes from their orifices. Scald them in hot water for 3-4 minutes. Allow to drain and put them aside.

Blanch the vine shoots and the tender wild carrot tops in boiling water for approximately 10 minutes at a high temperature. Add the snails, cover the pot and turn off the heat. Let the food boil until done. Remove with a skimmer and serve the food warm, sprinkled with abundant olive oil, salt and very little vinegar.

Snails with pligoùri

500gr snails

Olive oil

Fresh tomatoes

1 cup pligoùri

1 onion

1 glass wine

After washing the snails, scald them, sauté the onion, add the snails and the wine stirring continuously for 1 to 2 minutes. Add the grated tomatoes, some water and allow to boil over low heat. When it is almost done, stir in the *pligoùri*.

Snails with trahanàs

(serves 6)

1 kilo snails

1 cup EXTRA VIRGIN OLIVE OIL

1 onion

1 kilo potatoes

1 cup trahanàs

A little salt

Sauté the onion in olive oil and add the snails and potatoes in the pot. Cover with water and salt. Let them simmer. Just before the food is done, pour the *trahanàs* into the pot. Continue boiling for a while and then serve.

Anchovies in vinegar

(serves 10)

3 cups olive oil

1 kilo anchovies

2 cups vinegar

1 tablespoon table salt

Wash the anchovies and remove the intestines and the heads. Salt and place in a bowl. Add vinegar, cover with a dish and let stand for 4 hours.

Strain off the vinegar, slice lengthwise with a knife and remove the central bone. Immerse filets in vinegar again and let them stand for another 2 hours, until they turn white.

Next, remove from vinegar and place in a glass jar. Cover with olive oil and store in a cool place or in the refrigerator up to 5 - 6 months.

Anchovies with vinegar and garlic

(serves 10)

The recipe is executed in the same fashion as the previous one, the only difference being that you add 1 finely chopped clove of garlic in every 2 or 3 servings of anchovies when serving.

Roast anchovies with tomato and olive oil

1 kilo anchovies

2 large, ripe tomatoes

2 cloves of garlic

1 tablespoon oregano

1 cup EXTRA VIRGIN OLIVE OIL

Small lemon, juiced

Salt

Remove the head and the intestines of the anchovies and rinse thoroughly, clean and place in a fairly large baking pan. Sprinkle olive oil, lemon, salt and oregano on the fish. Then use your hands to mix well and add the garlic. Slice the tomatoes and use them to cover the anchovies. Finally, cook for 45-50 minutes at 180°C.

Marinated anchovies with roman pimpernel

1 kilo anchovies

1 cup salt, coarse grain

3 cups strong vinegar

2 cups roman pimpernel

1 cup olive oil

Remove the heads and the intestines from the anchovies. Rinse and salt thoroughly. Let stand for 2 hours, until all liquid is absorbed. Place them in a deep and narrow container or a big bowl and combine with coarse grain salt and enough vinegar to cover the anchovies. Set aside for 12 hours in this mixture. Remove the central bone and keep only the filets. Then place them in a glass jar, layering finely chopped roman pimpernel in-between. Cover with olive oil, seal and keep in a cool place or in the refrigerator.

When serving anchovies, sprinkle with a little more vinegar and a lot of finely chopped roman pimpernel.

Moray with tomato

1 kilo moray
1 cup olive oil
1-2 onions
1 bunch parsley
1/2 kilo tomatoes
Salt and pepper to taste

Wash and clean the moray. Sauté the onions with oil and add ground tomatoes, as well as finely chopped parsley. Season with salt and pepper and let boil for a while. Add the fish, stir and let it simmer, until the sauce thickens.

Moray pichti

1 moray, approx. 2 kilos
0.13gr saffron or 3-4 stamens
1 large onion, finely chopped
2 lemons, juiced
3 teaspoons olive oil
1/2 teaspoon savory
Salt
White pepper

Clean, wash and cut the fish into pieces. Next, salt it and put it in a pot with 8 glasses of water, olive oil and the onion to boil. Uncover the pot and boil for about 15 minutes at high temperature. Skim the froth off the top of the pot during boiling. Remove the pot from the fire, take the fish out with a skimmer and pass the broth through a thin colander.

Remove the bones from the fish very carefully and return it to its broth. Add the savory, pepper, lemon juice, the slightly grated saffron and a little salt or pepper, if needed. Boil the mixture again in an uncovered pot at high temperature and reduce by half.

Empty the mixture in deep dishes and place the *pichti* in the refrigerator for about 6 hours before serving.

Fish roasted on greaseproof paper

5 tablespoons EXTRA VIRGIN OLIVE OIL

1 big fillet of perch

2 cloves of garlic

1 teaspoon rosemary

Salt

Pepper, freshly ground

Wash and salt the fish. Spread out a double greaseproof paper and place the fillet in the centre. Sprinkle with garlic, rosemary and pepper. Pour olive oil over it and wrap in the greaseproof paper tightly.
Roast at 200°C for 45 minutes and serve hot with its gravy.

Roast fish ladorìgani

1 kilo fish

1 kilo potatoes

1 cup EXTRA VIRGIN OLIVE OIL

2 lemons, juiced

Salt, pepper, oregano

Clean the fish and slice it. Place on a baking pan, the sliced potatoes around it, season with salt, pepper and oregano and sprinkle with olive oil, lemon and a little water. Then bake at a moderate temperature for about an hour.

Roast fish

(serves 4)

1 cup EXTRA VIRGIN OLIVE OIL

4-5 slices dentex, white grouper, amberjack or tuna

2 medium-sized ripe tomatoes

1 tablespoon parsley, finely chopped

1 teaspoon lemon juice

Salt and pepper to taste

Wash the fish, cut into slices, salt and grill over charcoals or use an electric or oven grill. Finely chop tomatoes and combine with olive oil, parsley, lemon, salt and pepper.
Sprinkle with the prepared sauce and serve warm.

Grilled fish with fennel

1 - 2 bunches fennel

2 fish (half a kilo each)

Salt

For the sauce:

A small lemon, juiced

3/4 cup high quality olive oil

1 teaspoon fennel, finely chopped

3 tablespoons fresh tomato

Salt and pepper to taste

Layer the fennel on a grill. Clean and wash the fish very well. Salt inside and outside and place them over the layer of fennels on the grill with the burnt out charcoal.
Grill for 12 minutes and when the flesh starts to separate from the backbone, remove the fish from the grill and place on a serving plate. Clean the fish and sprinkle with the sauce which should be prepared as follows: put the olive oil, the lemon juice, tomato sauce, fennel in a big glass jar that seals well and season with salt and pepper. Seal the jar and shake well to obtain a uniform mixture.

Fish with courgettes

(serves 4)

1 kilo fish

1 kilo courgettes

1/2 kilo tomatoes

1 cup olive oil

1 onion

Salt and pepper to taste

Clean and salt the fish. Fry the courgettes slightly. Pour a little oil in a baking pan, place the fish in the middle and surround it with courgettes. Slightly simmer the rest of the oil with the onion and ground tomatoes and pour sauce and courgettes on top. Add 1 cup of water and some pepper and roast at a moderate temperature.

Monkfish (anglefish) with peppers

1 kilo fish

1 kilo peppers

1 cup olive oil

Salt and pepper to taste

Cut the peppers into rounds and layer half of them on a baking pan. Place the fish on top, season with salt and pepper and add the remainder of peppers on top. Sprinkle with olive oil and roast at a moderate temperature.

Cod with okras

1 kilo cod

1 kilo small okras

2-3 onions

4-5 cloves of garlic

1.5 glass olive oil

1 bunch parsley

700gr tomatoes

Salt and pepper to taste

Soak the cod in water and let stand to remove salt. Then remove the flesh and bones and place in the middle of a baking pan. Wash and clean the okras, fry them slightly and put them in the baking pan around the cod. Sauté the onion and garlic in the remaining oil in the frying pan, add ground tomatoes, salt and pepper and let the sauce boil for a while. Pour this sauce over the cod, sprinkle with a little parsley on top and cook the food, until only its oil remains.

Cod with cauliflower

1 cod filet

1 cauliflower

1 cup olive oil

1 onion

1 wine glass wine

1/2 kilo tomatoes

Salt and pepper to taste

Sauté onion with oil, add the cauliflower and extinguish with wine. Add the ground tomatoes, salt, pepper and a little water and let them boil for a while. Place the unsalted cod on top and finish cooking by tossing the pot a couple of times instead of stirring with a ladle.

Cod with sautéed greens

(serves 6)

1 kilo salt cod
1 kilo wild greens
1/2 kilo spinach
2 large onions
4 cloves of garlic
1 cup olive oil
2-3 ripe tomatoes
Salt and pepper to taste

Soak the cod overnight in water (replenish the water 2-3 times) and allow to stand in order to remove the salt prior to preparation. Then, cut into pieces. Rinse and clean the greens and spinach thoroughly. Sauté the finely chopped onions and garlic in olive oil until brown. Then gradually add the greens and spinach, until they shrivel. Afterwards add the ground tomatoes with a little salt and pepper and let them boil for about 20 minutes over moderate heat. Ten minutes before the vegetable is cooked, add the cod. You can also prepare the cod without tomatoes, if you wish.

Cod with green beans

1 cod filet

1 kilo green beans

1 cup olive oil

1 onion

1/2 kilo tomatoes

2-3 cloves of garlic

Pepper

Soak cod in water to remove the salt and cut it into bite-sized pieces. Clean and wash the green beans. Sauté the onions with the olive oil in a pot and add the green beans tossing the pot occasionally. Peel and finely chop the tomatoes, add garlic and pepper and let them boil for 15 minutes until done.

Cod with potatoes

1 kilo cod

1 cup olive oil

2 onions

1/2 kilo tomatoes

1 bunch parsley

1 kilo potatoes

Salt and pepper to taste

Sauté the finely chopped onions with oil and add ground tomatoes, parsley, salt and pepper. Let them boil for a while and then add the potatoes. Before they are done, add the unsalted cod and simmer for about 15 minutes.

Cod with lima beans

1/2 kilo lima beans

1 onion

1/2 kilo tomatoes

1 cup olive oil

1/2 kilo cod

Pepper

Boil the beans until half done. Strain and place them again in the pot with oil, onion and tomatoes. Cover them with water and before they are done, chop the soaked cod into medium-sized pieces and add it into the pot. Add a little pepper, let it boil for a while and serve.

Roast cod with wild leeks

1 kilo salt cod, cut into pieces (soak in water for 8 hours)

2 potatoes, sliced

1 sweet potato, sliced

4 cups leeks, finely chopped

3 cups white beets, finely chopped

4 tablespoons roman pimpernel, finely chopped

1 tablespoon fennel, finely chopped

1 cup spinach, finely chopped

1 bunch parsley, finely chopped

2 onions, cut into rounds

1 tablespoon tomato paste

2 tablespoons raisins

1 cup olive oil

Very little salt

Pepper, freshly ground

Wash and clean the vegetables meticulously under running water. Sauté the onions in a saucepan with olive oil for 3 minutes over moderate heat. Add the potatoes, sweet potato, greens, very little salt and a cup of water. Simmer for about 15 minutes and then add the raisins, tomato paste (dissolved in two tablespoons of water) and mix well.

In an oblong Pyrex dish, place the cod having soaked the salt out of it and lay the greens and potatoes on top. Add the gravy from the pot and place the baking pan on the bottom rack of the oven. Cook for 25 minutes at moderate temperature. Sprinkle with pepper and serve hot.

Fried swordfish with garlic

Some beer

Garlic

Cumin

Salt and pepper to taste

Flour

Fresh Mediterranean swordfish

Wash the swordfish. In a bowl pour some beer, crush a little garlic, add the cumin, salt, pepper, mix them all well and immerse the swordfish in this mixture. Next roll the fish in flour and fry over moderate heat. Serve the swordfish hot and accompany it with *skordaliá* and boiled greens.

Cuttlefish with fennel and green olives

(serves 6)

1 1/2 kilos cuttlefish, cleaned

5 spring onions, finely chopped

1 glass EXTRA VIRGIN OLIVE OIL

1 glass white wine

1/2 kilo fennels, finely chopped

5 tomatoes, grated

salt and pepper

1/2 kilo tsakistés green olives

Ink from three cuttlefish

2-3 cloves of garlic

Clean and cut the cuttlefish. Sauté with garlic and spring onion and extinguish with wine. Add the fennel, tomatoes, olives, salt, pepper and ink dissolved in 1/2 glass of water and boil over low heat for about 20 minutes.

Cuttlefish with olives

(serves 4)

1 kilo small cuttlefish

380gr small onions

250gr tsakistés olives or neratzoeliés

1 wine glass EXTRA VIRGIN OLIVE OIL

Salt and pepper

250gr firm red tomatoes

Rinse and clean the cuttlefish as required and cook them in their liquid. Add the wine and let boil. Add the salt, olive oil, pepper and grated tomatoes. Bring to a boil, clean the onions and add them either in half or whole, if very small. When the onions and the cuttlefish are almost done, add the olives. Cook over moderate heat. Serve with French fries.

Cuttlefish with wine

1 kilo cuttlefish

2-3 onions

1 cup olive oil

1 wine glass wine

Pepper

Clean the cuttlefish. Roughly chop the onion, sauté in olive oil and add the chopped cuttlefish. Cook for about a quarter of an hour until brown and then extinguish with wine. Add a little water and pepper and simmer cuttlefish, until only the oil remains.

Cuttlefish in their ink

(serves 4)

1 1/2 cups EXTRA VIRGIN OLIVE OIL

1 kilo fresh small cuttlefish

1 large onion

Clean the cuttlefish, remove the central bone, the intestines and the ink. Wash and chop them if they are large. Keep 3-4 ink bags. Next, heat the olive oil and sauté onion until brown. Then place the cuttlefish in the pot, slightly brown on all sides and add 2 cups of water. Cover the pot and let the cuttlefish simmer for 30 minutes. Then uncover the pot and add the ink bags, the salt and the wine. Continue boiling for 25-30 minutes until completely cooked.

Cuttlefish with spinach

1/2 kilo spinach

1 kilo cuttlefish or octopus

1 large onion, finely chopped

1 cup olive oil

1 lemon, juiced

Salt and pepper

Clean the cuttlefish, remove the intestines, bones and ink bags. Chop and sauté them with onion and olive oil, until slightly brown on all sides. Add 2 cups of water, reduce the temperature and simmer for about 45 minutes. Use a fork to check if cuttlefish is almost done.
Clean and cut spinach in thick pieces and add into the pot. Add a little salt and pepper, stir and let simmer with the lid on for 20-25 minutes. Pour the lemon juice over the food and stir. Serve warm or slightly cold.

Cuttlefish with spinach

1 kilo cuttlefish

1 kilo spinach

1 cup olive oil

2 onions or 5-6 spring onions

1 wine glass white wine

1 cup olives

Some dill or fennel, spearmint

Salt and pepper to taste

Clean the cuttlefish. Sauté the onions with the olive oil and add the dill or fennel, as well as the spearmint and finally the chopped cuttlefish. Bring to a boil, extinguish with wine and add the olives. Let the cuttlefish boil and when nearly done add the finely chopped spinach, a little salt, a little pepper and 1-2 glasses water. Boil for 10 more minutes. If the olives are salty, soak in water for some time to remove excess salt.

Cuttlefish with kritharàki pasta

1 kilo cuttlefish

1 cup olive oil

2 onions

3 ripe tomatoes

1/2 kilo kritharàki pasta

A little salt, pepper, 1 cinnamon stick

Clean and wash the cuttlefish. Sauté the finely chopped onions in oil and add the cuttlefish. Boil for a while and add the ground tomatoes, pepper and cinnamon. Boil the cuttlefish until done and afterwards add 3 1/2 parts water and 1 part kritharàki pasta in the pot. Bring to a boil and add the kritharàki pasta as well as a little salt. Let the kritharàki simmer, until all liquid is absorbed.

Cuttlefish or octopus with rice

1 kilo cuttlefish

1 glass olive oil

2 onions

3 ripe tomatoes

1/2 kilo rice

Salt, pepper, nutmeg

Clean and rinse the cuttlefish or octopus and sauté in olive oil with the onions. Boil for a while, add the ground tomatoes, salt, pepper and simmer for about an hour. Add the required amount of water in the pot (2.5 cups of broth for each cup of rice). Bring to a boil, add the rice and let boil stirring occasionally. Remove from heat, cover with a clean towel and leave aside for 10 minutes before serving.

Cuttlefish or octopus with potatoes

1 kilo cuttlefish

1 cup olive oil

1 onion

1 bunch fennel

1 kilo potatoes

3-4 large tomatoes

Salt and pepper to taste

Clean and wash the cuttlefish or octopus and sauté in olive oil with onions. Then add the finely chopped fennel and pepper. Cover them with 2-3 glasses of water and when nearly done add the finely chopped tomatoes, a little salt and potatoes cut into rounds. Let them boil, until their broth is absorbed.

Octopus with potatoes

1 octopus of approx. 1.5 kilos

Olive oil

Onion, finely chopped

Fennel

Pepper

Potato

Chop the octopus and boil it in a pot with a glass of water. When the water is absorbed, pour a glass of red wine. Cool, until wine is absorbed, add the oil and sauté the finely chopped onion. When the octopus begins to brown, pour 1.5 glasses of water and bring to a boil. Then, add the potato and fennel and cook them, until potato is done and only a little sauce remains. Serve the octopus hot and accompany with a glass of black wine.

Octopus with koftò macaroni

1 kilo octopus

1/2 kilo koftò macaroni

1 glass olive oil

1 onion

1/2 kilo tomatoes

1 wine glass wine

Salt and pepper to taste

Wash and chop the octopus. Sauté the onion in oil and boil the octopus in a pot for some time. Extinguish with wine and boil a little more. Then, add the ground tomatoes and pepper and boil well. Remove the octopus from the pot, add a little water and bring to a boil. Then add the koftò macaroni and cook until done. Serve on a platter with the octopus.

Octopus with black bryony

1 kilo octopus, chopped

2 bunches black bryony

2 large onions, finely chopped

1 cup olive oil

1 cup aromatic red wine

Salt and pepper

Wash the black bryony and remove the lower hard part. Boil for 10 minutes, remove with a skimmer and drain completely.
Slightly sauté the onion in olive oil and add the octopus. Stir, add the wine and 1 cup water, cover it and simmer for another 45 minutes. Check with a fork, if the octopus is done. Then add the black bryony and season with salt and pepper. Remove the lid and boil for another 20 minutes. Serve the food warm.

Octopus stifàdo

1 kilo octopus

1 cup olive oil

1 kilo onions

1 small cup vinegar

2-3 cloves of garlic

3-4 bay leaves

Pepper

Wash and chop the octopus. Sauté the onion with olive oil and add the octopus in the pot. Boil over low heat in its own gravy and when almost done add the garlic, vinegar, bay leaves, pepper, a little water, if necessary, and boil for a little while.

Boiled octopus in vinegar

1 kilo octopus

1 cup olive oil

2-3 cloves of garlic

1 small cup vinegar

Pepper, oregano

Wash the octopus well and clean it. Boil it in its own liquid over low heat. Wait until the liquid is absorbed and if the octopus is not yet done, add more water. When it is fully cooked (after one hour approximately) remove it from the pot and chop it. Beat olive oil with vinegar, finely chopped garlic, pepper and oregano and pour over the octopus. No salt is required. It can be kept in the refrigerator for several days.

Octopus with fennel and green olives

1 kilo octopus

1 kilo fennel

1 cup tsakistès green olives

1 cup olive oil

3 spring onions, finely chopped

2 large tomatoes, crushed

1/2 cup aromatic red wine

Very little salt

Pepper, freshly ground

Clean the octopus well. Boil the fennel in some water for 6 minutes, strain and finely chop. Slightly sauté the spring onions in olive oil in a pot. Add the chopped octopus and 2 cups of water and simmer for about 50 minutes. Use a fork to check whether the octopus is done or not. Then extinguish with wine and add fennel, tomatoes, salt and 1 extra cup of water. Continue simmering and add some more water, if required. Add the olives 10 minutes before removing the food from heat. Sprinkle with abundant freshly ground pepper and serve warm.

Octopus with olives

1 kilo fresh octopus

500gr small onions

250gr tsakistès olives

1 wine glass EXTRA VIRGIN OLIVE OIL

250gr firm red tomatoes

Salt and pepper

Cook the octopus in its liquid for some time. Extinguish with wine and add the olive oil, salt and the grated tomatoes. Bring to a boil and add the small onions peeled and cut into half or whole, if small. When half done, add the olives. Cover the pot and let the food boil. Simmer over moderate heat. Serve with french fries.

Grilled octopus on the charcoals

1 octopus

Olive oil

Vinegar

Salt

Pepper

Clean and wash the octopus and boil over low heat, until it absorbs its broth. Then remove from heat and strain, season with salt and pepper, brush with a little olive oil and place over charcoals. When done, arrange on a serving platter and sprinkle with oil, vinegar and oregano.

Octopus cooked in wine

1 kilo octopus

1 cup olive oil

1 glass red wine

1/2 kilo tomatoes

2-3 bay leaves, pepper

Wash and chop the octopus. Place it in a pot, add olive oil and let it boil, until the water evaporates. Extinguish with wine, add the ground tomatoes, bay leaves and pepper and let it boil, adding a little water, if necessary.

Squid with greens

1 kilo squid

1 cup olive oil

1-2 onions

2-3 cloves of garlic

1 bunch dill

1 kilo stewed greens (giachnerà) and spinach

1/2 kilo tomatoes or 2 lemons

Pepper

Clean and wash the squid. Place them in a pot without adding any water, as they will produce their own liquid. When their liquid is completely absorbed, add the olive oil, onions, the coarsely cut garlic, as well as the dill. Add a little water and boil. Then blanch the greens and add them into the pot. Pour the lemon juice or tomato and pepper and let them boil, until all liquid is absorbed.

Stuffed squid

(serves 4)

1 1/2 cups EXTRA VIRGIN OLIVE OIL

1 kilo medium-sized squid

1 large onion

2 spring onions

2 tablespoons dill, finely chopped

2 cups rice

2 tablespoons plums, finely chopped

1/2 teaspoon nutmeg

1 lemon, juiced

Salt and pepper to taste

Wash and clean the squid. Empty them by removing the central membrane. Remove the tentacles and finely chop them in a separate bowl. Add the onions, dill, rice, plums, 1/2 cup olive oil, nutmeg, a little salt and pepper. Stuff the squid with this mixture. Secure the end of each squid with a hard toothpick, so that the stuffing will not come out. Place in a wide pot, add 1 1/2 cups water, cover them and simmer for 30-40 minutes. Carefully take them out with a fork and place them in a Pyrex dish. Sprinkle them with the remainder of the olive oil and lemon. Place the squids in the oven for 20-30 minutes at moderate temperature until brown. Let them cool and serve.

Squid with tomato

1 kilo squid

1 cup olive oil

1-2 onions

1 bunch parsley

1/2 kilo tomatoes

Salt and pepper to taste

Wash and clean the squid. Sauté the onions in olive oil and add the ground tomatoes as well as the finely chopped parsley. Season with salt and pepper and let boil for a while. Add the squid, stir and simmer, until the sauce thickens.

Fried squid

Squid

Salt and pepper to taste

Olive oil and flour for frying

Clean and wash the squid. Cut and separate the tentacles and cut the ink bag in round ring-shaped slices. Season with salt and pepper, flour and deep-fry in plenty of hot oil.

Meat dishes

Hare stifàdo

1 hare

1 cup olive oil

1 kilo onions

1 glass white wine

5-6 ripe tomatoes

3-4 bay leaves

Salt, pepper, cumin

1 cinnamon stick

1 tablespoon vinegar

Chop the hare and place in a pot with oil, salt and wine. Boil for some time, add the coarsely cut onions, ground tomatoes, pepper, cumin and bay leaves and continue cooking until done. Add vinegar just before you turn off the heat.

Rabbit with yoghurt and eggs

1 rabbit

2 lemons

1 cup olive oil

2-3 tablespoons butter

1/2 kilo yoghurt

4 eggs

Salt and pepper to taste

Wash the rabbit, pour the lemon juice over it and let stand for several hours. Place in a baking pan, season with salt and pepper, sprinkle with olive oil, butter and some water and finally place it in the oven to bake. When done, remove from the oven, combine the yoghurt with the beaten eggs and 2-3 tablespoons water and pour this mixture over the rabbit. Transfer again into the oven, until the sauce sets.

Rabbit with endives avgolémono

1 medium-sized rabbit, chopped

2 bunches endives

4 spring onions

1 tablespoon dill, finely chopped

3/4 cup olive oil

2 lemons

2 eggs

Salt - pepper

Remove any yellow and wilted leaves from the endive. Wash them thoroughly and chop them. Slightly sauté the rabbit in olive oil. Add the spring onions, dill, a little salt and 2 cups water. Let meat simmer for about 30 minutes. Add the endives and 1 cup water and cook for 25 more minutes.

Beat the eggs and gradually stir in the lemon. Continue beating with a fork, stirring in a small amount from the food broth. Pour the egg-lemon *(avgolèmono)* sauce over it and slightly toss the pot over low heat. Serve the food warm.

Rabbit with oregano

1 rabbit

1 glass olive oil

2 lemons, juiced

1 head of garlic

Salt, pepper

2 teaspoons oregano

2 glasses water

Cut the rabbit into portions and place into pot with all ingredients. Let the food boil, until the sauce thickens.

Fried rabbit

1 rabbit

1 glass white wine

Some rosemary

3-4 cloves of garlic

Salt and pepper to taste

Flour and olive oil for frying

Cut the rabbit into portions, wash and place in bowl with wine, finely chopped garlic, rosemary, salt and pepper. Let stand in the wine for a few hours. Afterwards strain, flour and fry shortly on each side in hot olive oil.

Rabbit with rice

1 rabbit

1 onion

1 cup olive oil

1 wine glass red wine

2-3 ripe tomatoes

2 glasses rice

Salt and pepper to taste

Cut the rabbit into medium-sized pieces. Pour the olive oil in a pot and brown the rabbit with onion. Extinguish with wine, lower the heat and simmer. Add the ground tomatoes and finish off the boiling process. Then remove from the pot, pour 4 glasses of water and bring to a boil. Add rice, salt and pepper. After 10 minutes return the rabbit into the pot and turn off the heat.

Rabbit stuffed with mizìthra cheese

1 medium-sized rabbit

1 kilo mizìthra cheese

2 tablespoons butter

Oregano, salt, pepper

Season the rabbit and brush it with butter and stuff with the *mizìthra* cheese. Use a string to tie it shut or sew it with a thread and needle, wrap it in greaseproof paper and tie it again with a string. Roast at low temperature.

Rabbit with artichokes

1 rabbit

1 kilo potatoes

1/2 kilo courgettes

10 artichoke hearts

2 lemons, juiced

Salt and pepper to taste

Olive oil for frying

Slice the potatoes and slightly fry them, add the whole courgettes, the artichoke hearts scored into four and the rabbit cut into medium-sized pieces. Place all ingredients in a pot and sprinkle with olive oil, the juice of 2 lemons and 1-2 glasses of hot water. Season with salt and pepper, boil for some time and serve.

Rabbit with yoghurt

1 rabbit

1/2 cup butter

1/2 cup olive oil

1/2 kilo yoghurt

salt and pepper to taste

Stuff the abdomen of the rabbit with yoghurt and sew it. Then season with salt and pepper and spread butter and olive oil on top. Place it in a baking pan and roast for about 2 hours at a moderate temperature until brown on all sides.

Rabbit cooked in wine

1 rabbit

1 glass muscat wine

1 glass dry white wine

1/2 glass olive oil

1/4 kilo black olives

1/4 kilo ladotìri cheese

Salt and pepper to taste

Savory

Chop the rabbit and marinate in the wine for 1 day. Sauté the rabbit and extinguish with the marinade. Then add the olives and 1 glass of water. Add salt, pepper and savory. Let it boil for 1 hour. Just before it starts boiling, add the diced *ladotìri* cheese.

Rooster cooked in wine

(serves 6)

1 rooster

1/2 kilo white wine

5 tomatoes, grated

1 glass olive oil

1 onion

2 tablespoons parsley

Salt and pepper to taste

Sauté the rooster with the onion and garlic. Extinguish with the marinade and add the tomatoes, salt and pepper. Simmer for about 1 hour. Just before it starts boiling, sprinkle with the parsley.

Chicken with chestnuts

(serves 6)

1 chicken 1 1/2 kilos

2 medium onions

1 red pepper

2 kilos chestnuts

1 glass wine olive oil

1 glass red wine

Salt and pepper

Wash the chicken, cut it into portions, strain and season with salt and pepper. Then sauté in olive oil for 10 minutes and extinguish with wine. Chop the onions and pepper and add them into the pot. Sauté them for 2-3 minutes, add a little water and boil over moderate heat for 30 minutes. Then add the peeled and boiled chestnuts and let them boil for 10 more minutes. Instead of water add two grated ripe tomatoes, if you wish.

Baked chicken

1 chicken

2 cups breadcrumb

1 cup milk

Salt and pepper to taste

Cut the meat into big portions, season with salt and pepper, plunge each portion in milk and dip its entire surface in breadcrumbs. Lay a greaseproof paper on a baking pan and brush it with butter or olive oil. Then arrange the portions on top and bake without turning them over.

Baked chicken with cheese

1 chicken

1/2 kilo cheese (preferably graviéra cheese)

Butter, salt

Chop the chicken into medium pieces and boil. When done, cool and de-bone. Butter a baking pan, arrange the pieces of chicken and cover each one with a piece of *graviéra* cheese. Bake for a while, until the cheese melts.

Chicken with purslane

1 kilo purslane

1 kilo small courgettes

1 chicken, chopped

2 potatoes, quartered

2-3 fresh tomatoes, finely chopped

1 large onion, finely chopped

1/2 cup red wine

1 cup olive oil

Salt

Pepper, freshly ground

Sauté chicken and onion in olive oil until slightly brown. Extinguish with wine, add 2 cups water, cover and simmer for about 35 minutes.

Add the potatoes, a little more water, if required, and continue boiling for 15 minutes with the lid on. Add courgettes, purslane, tomatoes, salt, pepper and toss the pot in order to mix well all vegetables with the chicken. Simmer for 25-30 minutes, until only the oil remains. Serve somewhat warm or even cold.

Chicken with yoghurt

1 chicken

2 lemons

1 cup olive oil

2-3 tablespoons butter

1/2 kilo yoghurt, 4 eggs

Salt and pepper to taste

Wash the chicken, sprinkle with the lemon juice and allow to stand for several hours. Afterwards place it in the baking pan, season with salt and pepper, sprinkle with olive oil, butter and some water and bake in the oven. When done, remove from the oven, combine the yoghurt with the beaten eggs along with 2-3 tablespoons of water and pour the mixture over the chicken. Transfer again into the oven, until the sauce sets.

Chicken with oregano

1 chicken

1 cup olive oil

Olive oil for frying

1 onion

1 wine glass lemon juice

1 tablespoon oregano

Salt

Chop the chicken in medium-sized pieces and plunge it into water containing a handful of salt. Let it soak for 4 hours, take it out and remove the skin. Fry the chicken in olive oil until brown. Then place it in a pot with the olive oil, the quartered onion, lemon juice, oregano, some salt and cover it with water. Boil the chicken, until only the olive oil remains in the pot.

Chicken with okras

1 chicken

1 onion

1 kilo okras

5-6 large tomatoes

1 glass olive oil

1 teaspoon sugar

Lemon juice or vinegar

Cut the chicken and sauté in olive oil with the onion. When golden brown, add the peeled and finely chopped tomatoes in the pot, add salt, pepper, some water and simmer. When done, remove with a skimmer from the pot. Wash the okras, cut the stem ends and sprinkle with lemon juice or vinegar. Leave for 1-2 hours and afterwards place in the pot with some water, season with salt and pepper and 1 teaspoon sugar. Let the okras boil over moderate heat and do not stir, but simply toss the pot occasionally, so that the food does not stick and burn on the bottom.

Chicken with peas

1 chicken

1 cup olive oil

1/2 kilo peas

Salt

2 lemons, juiced

Cut the chicken into big portions, salt and place it on a baking pan with the skin facing downwards and sprinkle with a cup of olive oil or melted butter. Cover the baking pan with aluminium foil and put in the oven at 200°C. In approximately half an hour open the oven, uncover the baking pan, turn the portions over and sprinkle with lemon juice. When it is almost done, add the peas in between and bake for about 15 minutes.

Soudzoukàkia with olives

(serves 6)

1 kilo meat, fat removed

1 water glass wine

200gr bread or melba toast

1 small onion

2 cloves of garlic

Salt, pepper, a little cumin, a little cinnamon

2 eggs

100gr green olives

Soak the bread or melba toast in wine. Finely chop the onion and the garlic. Strain the soaked bread or melba toast and combine them with the minced meat. Then add the eggs, salt, pepper, cinnamon and the pounded cumin. Wet your hands with wine and mix the ingredients very well. Then, shape the *soudzoukàkia* and fry them. Prepare a red sauce with 1/2 kilo tomatoes and 2 tablespoons olive oil. Add the olives to the *soudzoukàkia* and simmer.

Pork baked in wine

1 boneless shoulder of pork

1 kilo white wine

1 sprig of rosemary

6-8 cloves of garlic

1 glass olive oil

Oregano, thyme

Salt

Ground pepper and whole black pepper

Marinate the shoulder for one day in a marinade of wine, rosemary, whole pepper, oregano, thyme and garlic. Arrange the meat on a baking pan. Cut slits with a knife and stuff each one of them with a piece of garlic. Sprinkle with salt and pepper, pour over some marinade and olive oil. Bake in the oven for about 2 hours at 180°C pouring the entire marinade at regular intervals.

Pork krassomezés

1 kilo meat	
2 cloves of garlic	
1/2 kilo tomatoes, peeled and finely chopped	
1 glass white wine	
Salt, pepper, cumin	

First sauté the garlic in some oil and then add the tomatoes and boil for a while. Extinguish with wine and add salt, pepper, cumin and chopped meat. Simmer.

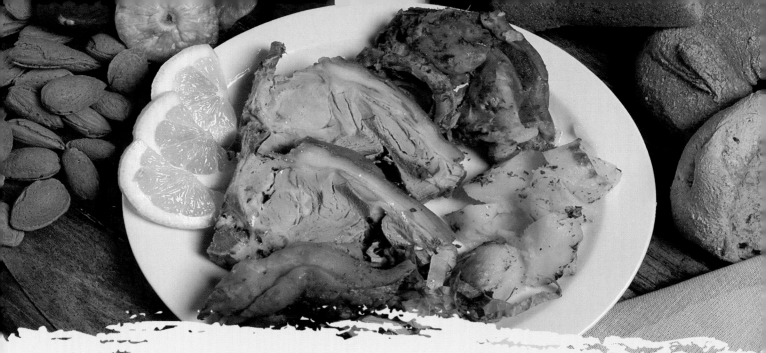

Pork with leeks and plums

1 kilo shoulder of pork, chopped

1 kilo leeks

5 tablespoons celery, finely chopped

8 plums, cut and halved

1 onion, small and finely chopped

1 tablespoon tomato paste

3/4 cup olive oil

Salt

Pepper, freshly ground

Slightly sauté the onion with the olive oil. Place pork in the pot and brown on every side. Add 1 cup of water, a little salt and simmer for about 30 minutes. Take the meat out and arrange on a platter. Place the leeks (cut into rounds), 2 cups of water and a little salt in the pot. Cook for 25 minutes at moderate temperature.

Return the meat to the pot, add the tomato paste (dissolved in a little tepid water), the plums and the celery. Stir and continue cooking, until the liquids are completely absorbed. Serve warm with plenty of freshly ground pepper.

Smoked pork omelette with black mustard

1/2 kilo black mustard

7 eggs

1 cup smoked pork ham from the thigh

1 cup kefalogravièra cheese, grated

1/2 cup milk

1/2 cup olive oil

1 teaspoon butter

Salt

Black pepper, freshly ground

Place the black mustard in plenty of boiling salted water. Boil until tender, take out with a skimmer and strain completely. Sauté the black mustard in olive oil for about 8 minutes. Then place in a bowl and add salt, pepper and the smoked pork.

Preheat the oven to 180°C. Beat the eggs with a fork, until they become frothy, add the milk, the cheese and continue beating for a few more minutes. Mix them with the greens-pork mixture and empty in a slightly buttered round vessel.

Bake at moderate temperature for 45 minutes.

Pork with olives

(serves 4)

1 kilo pork

250gr red firm tomatoes

500gr small round potatoes of equal size

250gr sweet green olives

1 wine glass EXTRA VIRGIN OLIVE OIL

Salt and pepper to taste

Brown the meat in the oil and extinguish with wine. Add the grated tomatoes, salt and pepper. Boil briefly, until the meat is half cooked. Add the potatoes and when done, add the olives and boil a while longer.

Pork with celery

1.5 kilo boneless pork

2 kilos celery, 2 onions

1 glass oil, 1/2 wine glass lemon juice

Salt and pepper to taste

Place the celery in a pot with water, boil and strain. Sauté the onion in oil and add the chopped pork. Add some water and cook meat for 45 minutes. Place the celery in the pot with salt and pepper and continue simmering. Do not stir with the ladle but toss the pot, so as the meat does not stick. When only the oil remains, add the lemon juice and serve.

Meat with eggplant

1 kilo meat (boneless pork, veal or lamb)

1 glass oil

1 kilo oblong eggplant

1 cup white wine

3-4 medium-sized tomatoes

2-3 cloves of garlic

Salt, pepper, 1 cinnamon stick

Cut the eggplant in medium-sized slices, salt them and let them sit for a while to get rid of their bitterness. Rinse, dry and slightly fry. Cut the meat into bite-sized pieces, sauté in oil and extinguish with wine. Add the tomatoes, garlic, some water, salt, pepper and cinnamon and simmer. When almost done, add the eggplant and boil together for a while.

Fried pork

1 kilo meat

1 wine glass wine

1/2 wine glass vinegar

Salt, pepper, oregano

1 glass olive oil

Wash and chop the meat into medium-sized pieces, season with salt and pepper, add oregano, sprinkle with vinegar and leave aside for a while. Heat oil in a frying pan and add the pork with its broth. Simmer over low heat, until the broth is absorbed and then add the wine. Continue simmering and when the wine is absorbed and the meat acquires a brown colour, turn the heat off.

Pilàfi rice from Hania

1 kilo lamb or kid and 1 chicken

1 wineglass lemon juice

5 tablespoons butter (stàka butter)

2 cups rice

6 cups stock

Salt

Boil the meat, strain and collect its stock. Measure the stock and pour it again in the pot to boil with the rice. When the rice is half done, add the lemon juice. Remove from heat. Heat some butter and pour over the rice. For 3 glasses of stock add 1 glass of rice. If the stock is not enough, add some water.

The *pilàfi* can be accompanied with yoghurt.

Kid with vine leaves

1 kilo kid, cut into medium-sized pieces

2 cups olive oil

2 bunches spring onions, finely chopped

2 bunches dill, finely chopped

300gr vine leaves, boiled

3 cups water

Salt and pepper

Brown the meat in olive oil with the onion and the dill, for 10 minutes. Add water and simmer for 20 minutes. Add the vine leaves and simmer for another 20 minutes.

Kid with spiny chicory

1 kilo kid, chopped

1 kilo spiny chicory

7 teaspoons olive oil

2 tablespoons white wine

2 lemons, juiced

Salt and pepper

Clean and wash the spiny chicory thoroughly. Immerse in boiled water for 5 minutes and blanch to offset its bitterness. Heat olive oil and brown the meat over moderate heat for 4 minutes. Extinguish with wine, salt, add 1 glass of water, cover and simmer for about 30 minutes.

Add the spiny chicory, stir, cover the pot and let the food simmer for 20 minutes. Add lemon juice, continue stirring and let the food boil for 5 more minutes. Serve warm in its rich sauce.

Kid with potatoes cooked in tomato sauce

1.5 kilo kid

1 kilo potatoes

1 small onion

1 kilo ripe tomatoes

1 cup olive oil

Salt and pepper to taste

First boil the meat in some water and when the water is absorbed pour the oil and sauté. Immediately add the onion and then the tomato and season with salt and pepper. When the meat is half done, remove it from the pot and add the potatoes. Before the potatoes are done, return the meat to the pot (keep the meat on one side of pot and potatoes on the other). Season with salt and pepper, add 2-3 glasses of water, cover the potatoes with a plate so as not to spread and let boil for 45 more minutes.

Baked kid with potatoes

1.5 kilo kid, preferably thigh

1 kilo potatoes

2-3 cloves of garlic

1/2 kilo tomatoes

1 glass red wine

1 cup olive oil

Salt and pepper to taste

Wash, chop the meat and then boil it in salt water. When half done, place it in a baking pan, sprinkle with garlic and pour the wine and the ground tomato on top. Add the oil, salt, pepper and meat broth and bake in the oven, until the potatoes are done.

Kid with golden thistle avgolémono

1 kilo kid

1 kilo golden thistle

1 large onion, finely chopped

1 cup olive oil

1 egg

2 lemons, juiced

Salt and pepper

Boil the golden thistle for 15 minutes in salted water. Take it out with a skimmer and strain. Reserve 5 cups of broth and use it in order to finish off the cooking process.
Slightly sauté the onion in olive oil. Add the chopped meat and brown it on all sides. Afterwards add 1 cup broth and simmer for 8 minutes. Add the golden thistle and the remainder of the broth, cover and cook over moderate heat for about 45 minutes. Season the food with salt and pepper and toss the pot to stir the food.

Remove the pot from heat and prepare the egg-lemon (avgolèmono) sauce by first beating the egg whites for 2 minutes. Then add the egg yolks and beat the mixture for a few more minutes. Add the lemon juice and gradually, in very small quantities, some of the food's sauce. Gradually pour the sauce in the pot, toss lightly, cover the pot and let it rest for 10 minutes before serving.

Kid with tsakistés green olives

1 kilo kid

1 cup olive oil

1 onion

1/2 kilo tomatoes, finely chopped

600gr tsakistés green olives

Lemon juice, pepper

Chop and salt the meat and then place it in the pot with olive oil. Let it boil for some time, add the onion and the finely chopped tomato. Continue boiling and then add the olives. If the broth is not enough for the food to cook through, add wine, until the food is thoroughly cooked. A few minutes before turning off the heat, take it off the fire and sprinkle with lemon juice.

Kid ladorìgani

(serves 6)

1 cup EXTRA VIRGIN OLIVE OIL

1 kid thigh, about 1 1/2 kilos

1 cup dry white wine

1 tablespoon oregano

1 tablespoon flour

1 teaspoon salt

Pepper

1 lemon, juiced

Chop the meat and simmer in a covered pot, until all water is absorbed.

Add the olive oil, stir, cook the meat until slightly brown and then extinguish with the wine. Dissolve the flour in 1 1/2 cups water and add in the pot with the oregano, salt, pepper and lemon. Place the lid on the pot and simmer for 30-35 minutes.

Serve in its gravy with french fries.

Lamb with Pilàfi in tomato soup

1 kilo lamb

1 cup olive oil

1 small onion, 1/2 kilo ripe tomatoes

2 glasses rice, salt, pepper

Chop the meat and de-bone. Then sauté the meat in the oil with the onion. Add some water or broth and simmer. Then add the ground tomatoes, season with salt and pepper and boil until done. In the meantime, soak the rice in a bowl with boiled water and 1/2 handful salt and scald for half an hour, otherwise the rice may become sticky (the quantity of rice should be half the quantity of the stock). Then rinse and pour into the pot with the meat. When it starts boiling, lower the heat and cover the pot. Simmer, until the broth is completely absorbed. Remove from the heat, stir and serve immediately.

Sautéed lamb

1 kilo lamb

100-150gr olive oil

Oregano

Pour the olive oil in a pot and when it burns, place the chopped meat and stir continuously until brown. Lower the temperature and cook the meat adding water, if required. When done, turn up the heat stirring continuously, until the olive oil starts foaming. At the end, sprinkle with oregano and serve.

Stewed or sautéed Sfakianò

(ingredients for 6 servings)

1 1/2 kilos two-year-old lamb (front part, not thigh)

2 cups olive oil

Salt and pepper to taste

Thoroughly rinse the meat, chop and allow it to stand in a bowl for 2-3 hours, so as to strain. Pour the olive oil in a pot and before it burns add the meat. Turn the heat up and stir continuously, until the meat acquires a whitish colour. Then season slightly with salt and pepper, cover the pot, reduce the heat to low and simmer for 1 1/2- 2 1/2 hours without adding any water.

Lamb with fennel

1 kilo lamb

1 kilo fennel

2 lemons

1 cup olive oil

Salt and pepper to taste

Pour the olive oil in the pot and sauté the meat. Immediately add the chopped fennel and boil well. Finally, add the lemon juice, salt and pepper. Let the food boil and serve.

Lamb with courgettes

1 cup olive oil

1 onion or 1-2 pieces of leek

1 kilo lamb

1 kilo courgettes, 1/2 kilo ripe tomatoes

Salt and pepper to taste

Sauté the meat with the onion or leek in olive oil. Add half of the tomatoes, cover the meat with water, salt, pepper and courgettes and let everything boil very well. When almost done, add the rest of the tomato. Cook thoroughly, until the sauce thickens.

Lamb with chicory

1 kilo wild chicory, finely chopped

1 kilo shoulder of lamb, chopped

2 onions, finely chopped

2 ripe tomatoes, finely chopped

3/4 cup olive oil

1 teaspoon dry coriander (crushed)

4 grains pimento

Salt

Pepper, freshly ground

Sauté the onions in olive oil until slightly brown and add the chopped meat. Sauté a little more, until the lamb turns golden brown. Add the salt, coriander, pimento and 2 cups of water. Stir, cover the pot and simmer for about 40 minutes. Try the meat with a fork. When it is almost done, add the chicory, the tomatoes, a little water, stir and boil further for 20-30 minutes.

Serve the food with freshly ground black pepper.

Lamb fricassee with spiny chicory

1 kilo lamb

500gr spiny chicory

100gr olive oil

1 onion

1 egg yolk

2 lemons

Salt and pepper to taste

White wine

Place the onion with the olive oil in a pot and sauté. Add the lamb and then the wine and stir, until the alcohol evaporates and only its fragrance remains.

Reduce the heat and add water, until the meat is done.

Boil the spiny chicory in another pot and when done, mix with the meat.

Whisk the egg yolks with the lemon juice and gradually stir in the mixture into the pot.

Lamb with okras

1 kilo lamb

1 kilo okras

1/2 kilo tomatoes

1 glass olive oil

1 onion, some vinegar, salt, pepper

Wash the okras, cut the stems, sprinkle with vinegar and dry in the sun for a while. Place the meat in the pot with the olive oil, sauté and then add the peeled and finely chopped tomatoes and let them boil for some time until the meat is half cooked. Place the okras in the pot, season with salt and pepper, pour a little water, if necessary, and cook thoroughly.

Lamb with asparagus avgolémono

1 kilo lamb

1 kilo asparagus

1 cup olive oil

1 onion, 1 lemon

salt and pepper to taste

1 tablespoon flour

Wash and chop the meat. Sauté in oil and onion, add the water and boil until half done. Clean the asparagus and boil for 5 minutes in salted water. Then combine them in the pot with the underdone meat and let cook. A few minutes before turning off the heat dissolve the flour in lemon juice and some broth from the pot and add this mixture to the food. Boil for another 2-3 minutes.

Lamb with vine shoots

1 kilo lamb

1 cup olive oil

1/2 kilo tender vine shoots

1/2 kilo chicory

1 small bunch fennel

1 bunch spring onions

1 small bunch parsley

2 eggs, 2 lemons, salt, pepper

Sauté the meat in oil for a while, add the fennel and water and simmer. Scald the vine shoots and the chicory in boiling water and when the meat is half done, combine the greens in the pot together with the finely chopped parsley, the coarsely cut onions and a little water. Boil until completely cooked and then turn the heat off, prepare the egg-lemon (*avgolèmono*) sauce and sprinkle over the food.

Lamb with yoghurt

1 kilo lamb, boneless

500-600gr strained yoghurt

2 bunches dill

2 bunches spring onions

Cumin

100gr olive oil

Oregano

Chop the lamb in bite-sized pieces. Finely chop the spring onions and the dill. Mix all the ingredients and bake in an earthenware casserole at 180°C.

Baked lamb with tomato

1 kilo lamb

2 lemons, juiced

2 tablespoons oil or butter

2-3 large tomatoes

Salt and pepper to taste

Cut the meat into portions, season with salt and pepper and place the pieces very close to each other in a baking pan. Sprinkle with lemon and oil or butter and cover with tomato slices. Roast in the oven and towards the end turn the heat up to ensure that the sauce thickens.

Roll of lamb with white beets

2-3 kilos lamb back

1 1/2 kilos white beets, finely chopped

4 spring onions, finely chopped

2 tablespoons spearmint

1 cup spicy kefalograviéra cheese, grated

1 tablespoon breadcrumb

2 cups lamb liver, finely chopped

3 teaspoons olive oil

1/2 cup dry white wine

Salt

Pepper, freshly ground

For the sauce:

1 lemon, juiced

2 cloves of garlic, crushed

2 teaspoons olive oil

In a deep frying pan sauté the onions in olive oil for 2-3 minutes. Add the liver and continue sautéing for 5 minutes stirring continuously. Season with salt and pepper and extinguish with wine. Let the mixture absorb its liquids and dry completely.

Let it cool completely, transfer to a deep bowl and mix with the white beets, the spearmint, the cheese and the breadcrumb. Season the inner part of the lamb back with salt and pepper and stuff it. Roll and wrap it tightly with a white cotton thread and place the roll on the oven grill. Roast at 200°C for 25 minutes, brushing regularly with a sauce made from olive oil, lemon juice and garlic.

Lower the heat to 180°C and continue roasting for 45 more minutes, until brown. Then remove from the oven, set aside to cool, cut the string and slice.

Serve warm.

Lamb on vine twigs

1 kilo lamb

1 glass white wine

2 lemons, juiced

Oregano

Vine twigs

Arrange the vine twigs on a baking pan. Place the lamb on top, pour the wine over it and roast at 180°C. Just before it is done, sprinkle with oregano and lemon juice.

Lamb with mizìthra cheese

1.5 kilo lamb

1 kilo mizìthra cheese

Salt and pepper to taste

Score the lamb, season with salt and pepper and bake at moderate temperature. When nearly done, cover with the *mizìthra* cheese and bake thoroughly.

Lamb with artichokes

1 kilo lamb

10 artichokes (hearts)

1 cup olive oil

1 bunch spring onions

1 small bunch dill or fennel

Salt, pepper

2 eggs

2 lemons

Sauté the meat in oil, add some water and simmer. Peel the artichokes and place in a bowl with water, salt, lemon and some flour so as not to darken. While the meat is still underdone, finely chop the artichokes, the spring onions, the dill or the fennel and add them in the pot. Cover the food in the pot with some water. Do not open the pot but toss occasionally, otherwise the artichokes will become discoloured. When the food is done, prepare the egg-lemon (avgolèmono) sauce, pour over the food, cool and serve.

Small pies with heather honey and walnuts

1 kilo flour (self-rising)

400g heather honey

3 teaspoons thyme honey

1 teaspoon cinnamon, ground

1 teaspoon nutmeg

1 cup nuts, coarsely ground

2 cups baking powder

1 cup orange juice

1/2 cup olive oil

1/2 cup sesame seeds

Blend the olive oil with the heather honey and the thyme honey for 2-3 minutes in the mixer at medium speed. Add the orange juice, the nutmeg, the cinnamon. Mix the flour with the baking powder and pour it in the mixer bowl as well. Blend for 5-6 minutes into a uniform, relatively thin mixture. Stir in the nuts and scatter evenly into the mixture. Empty the finished mixture into small, slightly oiled cake tins.

Dredge their surface with plenty of sesame seeds and bake at 180°C on the centre rack of the oven for 45-50 minutes. Remove from the baking tins, when completely cold.

Tiganòpita with almonds and sesame

For the dough

1 kilo flour

1 glass olive oil

1 lemon /orange, juiced

1/2 teaspoon salt

Some water

Olive oil for frying

For the filling

2 glasses almonds, roughly ground and browned

1 glass sesame seeds

1 cup sugar

Cinnamon and cloves, 1 teaspoon

For the syrup

1 glass honey

Cinnamon

1 glass sugar

1 glass water

In a bowl beat the oil, the salt and the lemon juice. Slowly pour in the flour and some hot water and work into a soft dough. Roll out a thin pastry sheet and cut into 8cm wide and 20cm long strips. Layer 2 teaspoonfuls of the filling on top, fold over and press edges together making sure that it is completely closed. Starting at one end, twist the ribbon in a spiral, similar to a *sarìki* (the traditional headdress of Cretan men). When the pastry sheet and the filling are used up, fry them. Pour the syrup on top and serve.

Tiganòpita

1 kilo flour

1 glass olive oil

1 lemon/orange, juiced

1/2 teaspoon salt

Some water

Honey, cinnamon

Olive oil for frying

In a bowl beat the oil, the salt and the lemon juice. Slowly pour in the flour and some hot water and work into a soft dough. Roll out a thin pastry sheet and cut circles in the size of a saucer. Fry them in hot oil until golden brown. Dissolve the honey in water (1 glass of water for each glass of honey) and pour over the pies. Sprinkle them with cinnamon and serve.

Bourekàkia

For the filling

1 kilo mizìthra cheese

5 tablespoons flour

2 tablespoons butter

1 cup milk

3 tablespoons sugar

1 tablespoon cinnamon

1/2 kilo phyllo pastry

For the syrup

1 cup sugar

1 glass water

1 wine glass cognac

1 small cup lemon juice

Some cinnamon

Heat the butter in a skillet and pour in the flour. Remove mixture from heat and let it cool. Next, pour in the milk, add the *mizìthra* cheese, the sugar and the cinnamon and stir well, until you have a smooth mixture. Lay 2-3 pastry sheets, spread the filling on top and fold them into the shape of a *sarìki*. Bake them in the oven until golden brown. Then, take them out and let them cool. Prepare the syrup and pour over the cool patties.

Bouréki

For the dough

1/2 kilo flour

1 small cup olive oil

1 lemon, juiced

1 glass milk

Some salt

For the filling

1 kilo sweet mizìthra cheese

3-4 tablespoons sugar

2 eggs

cinnamon or vanilla

lemon/orange rind, freshly grated

Mix all the ingredients for the pastry sheet and knead into a smooth dough. Roll out 3 pastry sheets. Lay the first pastry sheet on a buttered baking pan. Dredge with sugar and cinnamon and place it into a preheated oven for 10 minutes. Bake for a while. Next, spread half of the *mizìthra* cheese on top and lay out another pastry sheet. Dredge again with sugar and cinnamon and layer the rest of the *mizìthra* cheese. Top with the last pastry sheet. Dredge again with sugar and sprinkle with 3 tablespoons of melted butter. Bake the bouréki patty in the oven. When it is slightly baked, sprinkle with a cup of milk and continue baking until done.

Pies from Sfakià

(serves 10)

1/2 kilo flour

2 teaspoons olive oil

Salt

1 small glass tsikoudià

1 glass water

1/2 kilo mizìthra cheese

Knead the flour with the olive oil, the salt and
as much water as it takes into a soft dough.
Divide it into 10 pieces and roll them out into
pastry sheets in the shape of saucers.
Shape the *mizìthra* cheese into 10 balls, each
in the size of a large egg. Place the *mizìthra*
cheese in the middle of the pastry sheet. Fold
the pastry sheet around to cover the *mizìthra*
cheese. Continue in this fashion in order
to shape 10 small balls. Flatten them out by
means of a rolling pin and give them a round
shape in the size of a saucer.
Fry in a pan without oil, turning them over
frequently so that they do not burn.
Pour honey over each one before serving.

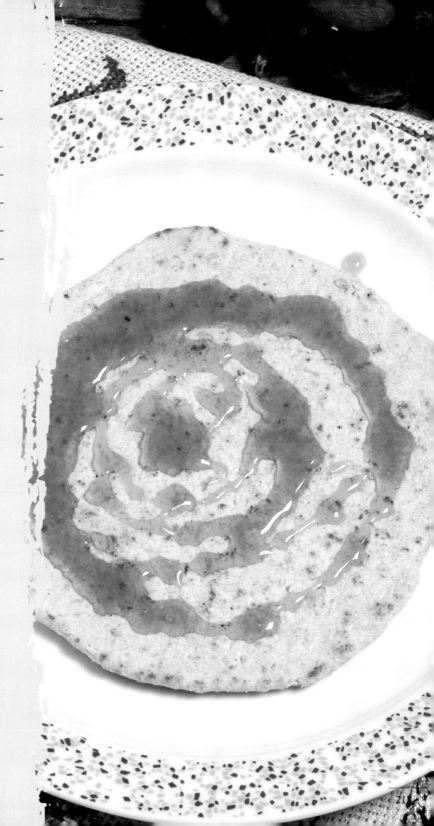

Katiméria from Sélino

For the dough

1 small cup olive oil

1 small cup tsikoudià

1 teaspoon salt

1 glass water

ca. 1/2 kilo flour

For the filling

1 plate homemade cheese, grated

3-4 eggs

2 teaspoons sugar

Combine the ingredients for the pastry sheet and knead into a firm dough. Prepare the filling with the cheese, the eggs and the two teaspoons of sugar. Roll out a pastry sheet and cut into circles, half of them in the size of a larger saucer and half of them in the size of a smaller saucer. Place the smaller pastry sheet on top of the larger one, so that you obtain a more solid bottom. Spoon some filling on the small pastry sheet and fold all sides over the filling so as to cover it. Fry them in plenty of olive oil without turning them over. Dredge with sugar and serve.

Baklavàs

For the pastry

1/2 kilo phyllo pastry

For the filling

2 cups almonds, coarsely chopped

2 cups nuts, croarsely chopped

2 teaspoons cinnamon

1 teaspoon clove

1 cup butter

For the syrup

3 cups sugar

2 cups water

1/2 cup honey

2 tablespoons lemon juice

vanilla extract

Mix the nuts, the almonds, the cinnamon and the cloves. Melt the butter, butter a baking tin and lay four buttered phyllo sheets. Spread some filling and layer 2 buttered phyllo sheets on top. Repeat the same procedure, until all sheets and filling has been used. Top off with 4 phyllo sheets. Cut the baklavà into square pieces, pour the rest of the butter on top and bake at moderate temperature until golden brown. Meanwhile, boil the syrup and pour it hot over the warm baklavà.

Patoùda

For the dough:

3 glasses olive oil

1 glass sugar

1 glass milk

1 wine glass tsikoudià

2 teaspoons ammonia

2 eggs

1 coffee cup aloussià (boil the water with one tablespoon ash and drain it)

For the filling:

1/2 glass water

1 teaspoon nutmeg

1 kilo walnuts and almonds, crushed

1 glass sugar

1 glass honey

2 glasses ground sesame seeds

Mix the ingredients for the pastry sheet and knead into a soft dough. Prepare a syrup with the sugar, the honey and the water and next, pour in the rest of the ingredients for the filling.

Divide the dough into small balls, roll them out, make a hole in the middle and place 1 teaspoon filling on them. Reshape into balls resembling a *kourabiés*. Bake at moderate temperature until golden brown. Cool and sprinkle with confectioner's sugar.

Dark amigdalotà

2 glasses almonds, crushed

1 1/2 glasses sugar

3 eggs

3 tablespoons rusk, grated

2 tablespoons cocoa

1 tablespoon cinnamon

Combine all the ingredients and mix well; shape the almond macaroons; place them on an oiled greaseproof paper. Top each one of them with 1/2 almond and bake them in the oven for 10 minutes.

Rice pudding in the oven

2 kilos milk

1 glass rice

1 glass sugar

450g butter

10 eggs

Beat the sugar with the butter until frothy. Slowly pour in the beaten egg yolks and continue to beat constantly by gradually adding the milk with the rice. Finally, beat the eggs until fluffy and add them to the mixture. Bake at a moderate temperature.

Karidotà

3 glasses walnuts

1 glass breadcrumbs

7 eggs

2 cups cognac

2 1/2 glasses sugar

1 teaspoon baking soda

1 teaspoon cinnamon and cloves

Confectioner's sugar

Beat the egg yolks with the sugar. Beat the egg whites until stiff and combine them with the rusk, the baking soda dissolved in 1 cup cognac, the cinnamon, the cloves and the ground walnuts. Stir and shape the walnut macaroons. Place them on a baking tin, brush them with butter and bake them at a moderate temperature for about 15 minutes. In the end, sprinkle them with the rest of the cognac and dredge them with confectioner's sugar.

Orange cookies

1 glass olive oil

1 glass sugar

1 1/2 glasses orange juice

2 teaspoons baking soda

2 wine glasses tsikoudià

Flour, as much as it takes

Combine all the ingredients and knead into a dough. Shape them into cookies and bake them at a moderate temperature.

Cookies from Sfakià

2 kilos flour
2 1/2 glasses olive oil
2 glasses sugar
1 glass orange juice
2 glasses water
2 teaspoons baking powder
1 tablespoon cinnamon
1 tablespoon cloves
Browned sesame seeds

Combine the oil with the sugar in a large bowl and stir well. Add the water, the baking powder dissolved in orange juice, the cinnamon, the cloves and finally, add the flour slowly, constantly working the mixture into a soft dough. Shape the cookies, sprinkle with sesame seeds and bake them at a moderate temperature.

Oil cookies

3 cups olive oil
2 cups sugar
2 cups cinnamon, boiled
1 packet baking powder
1/2 packet ammonia
2 kilos flour
Sesame seeds

Combine all the ingredients in a bowl and knead very well into a dough. First put the olive oil with the sugar in the bowl, then the cinnamon, the baking powder, the ammonia and, finally, the flour. Shape the cookies, sprinkle with some liqueur, sprinkle with sesame seeds and bake them at a moderate temperature.

Oil cookies with wine

2 glasses olive oil
1 1/2 glasses sugar
1 1/2 glasses white wine
1/2 glass orange juice
1 1/2 teaspoons baking soda
1 1/2 teaspoons baking powder
1 tablespoon cinnamon and cloves
1 1/2 kilos flour
Browned sesame seeds

Combine the olive oil with the sugar in a large bowl and stir well. Add the wine, the orange juice, the baking soda, the baking powder, the cinnamon and the cloves. Then, stir in the flour gradually. Knead very well, shape cookies, place them into the baking tray, dredge with sesames seeds, and finally, bake them.

Anise cookies

2 glasses olive oil
3 glasses sugar
1 glass water
1 glass orange juice
2 teaspoons baking soda
2 teaspoons cinnamon and cloves
1 teaspoon anise
2 1/2 kilos flour

Knead all ingredients well into a dough and proceed with shaping the cookies. Bake them at a moderate temperature.

Xerotìgana

1 kilo all purpose flour

2 tablespoons honey

1 egg

1 water glass sugar

1 cup milk

Sesame seeds

1/2 cup tsikoudià

1 glass water

Olive oil (for frying)

Cinnamon

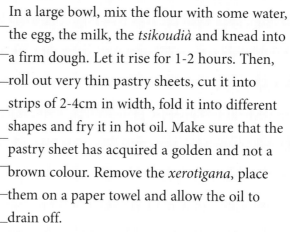

In a large bowl, mix the flour with some water, the egg, the milk, the *tsikoudià* and knead into a firm dough. Let it rise for 1-2 hours. Then, roll out very thin pastry sheets, cut it into strips of 2-4cm in width, fold it into different shapes and fry it in hot oil. Make sure that the pastry sheet has acquired a golden and not a brown colour. Remove the *xerotigana*, place them on a paper towel and allow the oil to drain off.

Next prepare the syrup (for 10-15 *xerotigana*) as following:

Combine the water and the sugar in a skillet, stir constantly and boil for 10-15 minutes, until the mixture sets. Remove from heat, add the honey and stir constantly, so that it does not stick. Afterwards, insert a toothpick in each *xerotigano*, dip them into the syrup and let them soak for 1-2 minutes. Arrange them on a platter and sprinkle lightly with sugar and cinnamon. If you wish, add some browned sesame seeds. Make sure that the oil in the frying pan covers the *xerotigana*, so that they are deep-fried.

Avgokalàmara

For the avgokalàmara

5 eggs

5 tablespoons oil

5 tablespoons sugar

5 tablespoons tsikoudià for dredging

1 glass milk

1 packet baking powder

Flour

For the syrup

2 glasses sugar

1 glass water

cinnamon, walnuts and sesame

Beat the olive oil with the sugar, the *tsikoudià*, the eggs, the milk and the baking powder. Slowly add the flour and knead well. Roll out a 1/2cm thick pastry sheet, cut it into squares of 10x10cm, twist them up in the shape of a cone, or tie them into knots. You can create all kinds of shapes and deep-fry them in hot oil. Then, place them on a paper towel. Prepare the syrup and immerse the *avgokalàmara* in the boiling syrup. Allow each one to soak for a while and then place them on a platter. Sprinkle with sesame seeds, cinnamon, coarsely ground walnuts and some sugar.

Lenten kourabiédes

640g olive oil

1 cup sugar

3/4 glass orange and tangerine juice

1 teaspoon baking soda

1 wine glass water

2 tablespoons cinnamon and cloves

Flour, as much as it takes

Rose water, confectioner's sugar

Beat the olive oil with the sugar and continue with the baking soda dissolved in orange juice, the cinnamon, the cloves and the flour. Knead into a soft dough, shape it into balls and flatten them. Then lay the kourabiédes on a baking tray and bake them. Let them cool, sprinkle them with rose water and sprinkle them with confectioner's sugar.

Melomakàrona

For the dough

4 glasses olive oil

1 1/2 glasses sugar

1 wine glass cinnamon, boiled

1 glass lemon and orange juice

2 teaspoons of baking soda

1 wine glass tsikoudià

1 teaspoon baking powder

Flour, as much as it takes

For the syrup

1 glass honey

1 glass sugar

1 glass water

1 cinnamon stick

Sesame seeds

Cinnamon

Beat the olive oil with the sugar. Then, add the cinnamon, the baking soda dissolved in orange juice, the baking powder dissolved in *tsikoudià* and the flour. Then, form oval shaped cookies and bake them at a moderate temperature. Let them cool. Meanwhile boil the syrup over low heat and immerse the *melomakàrona* in it. Let them soak for one minute and then remove them and place them on a serving platter. Sprinkle the *melomakàrona* with cinnamon and sesame seeds.

Melomakàrona with walnuts

For the dough

2 glasses olive oil

1 glass sugar

1/2 glass water

1 tablespoon honey

1 glass orange juice

and cinnamon for dredging

1 teaspoon baking soda

Orange rind, freshly grated

1 teaspoon cinnamon and cloves

1 teaspoon ammonia

1 glass walnuts, coarsely ground

Flour, as much as it takes

For the syrup

1 glass water

1 glass sugar

1 glass honey

walnuts, coarsely ground

Beat the olive oil with the sugar; then add the water, the cinnamon, the cloves, the baking soda dissolved in orange juice, the honey, the grated orange rind, the walnuts and the flour and knead into a soft dough. Then, form oval shaped cookies and bake them at a moderate temperature. Let them cool. Meanwhile boil the syrup over low heat and immerse the *melomakàrona* in it. Let them soak for one minute and then remove them and place them on a serving platter. Sprinkle the *melomakàrona* with cinnamon and walnuts.

Loukoumàdes

For the dough

2 cups water

2 cups flour

1 cup olive oil or butter

1 teaspoon salt

2 cinnamon sticks

lemon rind, grated

For the syrup

2 cups sugar

1 cup water

2-3 teaspoons honey

6 eggs

2-3 cloves

2 teaspoons baking soda

lemon rind, grated

Place water, baking soda, salt, butter, cinnamon and grated lemon rind into a skillet and boil for 1-2 minutes. Pour in the flour and stir constantly with a wooden ladle, until the mixture starts to detach from the walls of the skillet. Remove the skillet from the fire, let cool for a while and add the eggs while stirring constantly. Heat the oil in a skillet; spoon small balls of dough using a wet spoon so that the dough does not stick and place them in the oil. Fry them until golden brown, take them out with a perforated skimmer and transfer them onto a serving plate.

Prepare the syrup by combining all ingredients in one skillet. Boil for 10 minutes, remove the cinnamon, the cloves and the grated lemon rind and add a wine glass of cognac. Pour the syrup over the *loukoumàdes*. Instead of syrup, you can use confectioner's sugar mixed with cinnamon to dredge the *loukoumàdes*.

Gooseberry marmalade

3 kilo gooseberries

1 kilo sugar

3 tablespoons lemon juice

2 pieces lemon rind

Wash and carefully peel the gooseberries. Cut their pulp into pieces and let them boil in a pot with some lemon rinds. Boil over low heat for about 20 minutes and stir constantly. Then, add the sugar and continue boiling skimming the froth rising on the surface. When the marmalade starts thickening, add the lemon juice, stir well and continue boiling for another 10 minutes. Let the marmalade cool, pour into airtight glass jars and seal well. Keep the marmalade in a cool place or the fridge for up to 8 months.

Quince marmalade

1 kilo quinces

800g. sugar

3 tablespoons lemon juice

2 pieces lemon rind

Wash and carefully peel the quinces. Cut their pulp into pieces and let them boil in a pot with some lemon rinds. Boil over low heat for about 20 minutes and stir constantly. Then, add sugar and continue boiling skimming the froth rising on the surface.

When the marmalade starts thickening, add the lemon juice, stir well and continue boiling for another 10 minutes. Let the marmalade cool, pour into airtight glass jars and seal well. Keep the marmalade in a cool place or the fridge for up to 8 months.

Bergamot marmalade

1 kilo bergamot

1 kilo sugar

3 tablespoons lemon juice

2 pieces lemon rind

Wash and carefully peel the bergamots. Cut their pulp into pieces and let them boil in a pot with some lemon peels. Boil over low heat for about 20 minutes and stir constantly. Then, add sugar and continue boiling skimming the froth rising on the surface. When the marmalade starts thickening, add the lemon juice, stir well and continue boiling for another 10 minutes. Let the marmalade cool, pour into airtight glass jars and seal well. Keep the marmalade in a cool place or the fridge for up to 8 months.

Quince preserve

1 kilo quinces, peeled

1/2 kilo sugar

1 glass water

Lemon rinds

Geranium (for flavouring)

1 lemon, juiced

Wash the quinces well, peel them and remove the hard part in the heart containing the cores. Slice them and chop them into small and narrow pieces. Combine all the ingredients in a pot: the quinces, the sugar, the water, the lemon rinds, and some leaves of geranium. Boil them over high heat, stirring constantly and when the mixture starts boiling, reduce the heat. Continue boiling for another 1/2 hour over low heat in an uncovered pot. Check if the syrup has thickened, pour over the lemon juice and remove the preserve from the heat.

Quince paste

1 kilo quinces

sugar, as much as required

Wash the quinces very well and quarter them. Then, peel, core and cut each quarter into 2-3 pieces. Collect the peels and the cores, place them in a perforated cotton fabric (*touloupàni*), tie it securely and immerse it into a pot with water. Add the quinces inside and let them boil until soft. Afterwards, mash them and pass them through the *touloupàni* three times.

Combine the sugar and the juice in a pot (1 cup of sugar for 1 cup of juice) and add 1 extra glass of juice. Boil it and check for doneness by placing a couple of drops in a glass of water or on a saucer; if the drop is not dissolved in the glass or does not stick on the saucer (after approximately 1 hour over low heat), then the paste is done. Before removing the paste from the fire, pour lemon juice over it.

Bitter orange preserve

1.5 kilo bitter orange rinds

2 kilo sugar

1 lemon, juiced

Grate the bitter orange rinds lightly to remove outer coat. Rinse and cut the rind into three or four pieces each. Remove and discard their pulp. Roll up the rinds and use a needle and thread to fasten them tightly so as to prevent them from unrolling. Subsequently, boil them, replenish the water and continue with the boiling process, until they soften. Soak them in water for two days, make sure you change the water regularly and let them stand, until they lose their bitter taste. Next take them out of the water and spread them on a towel to dry.

Place them again in the pot with the sugar and 1 glass water. Boil, until the syrup thickens. Before removing the preserve from heat, add the lemon juice. Make sure that the syrup almost covers the preserve, as it is quickly absorbed.

GLOSSARY

Akràtisma: Bread dipped in a glass of unalloyed [àkratos] wine, usually consumed for breakfast.

Àrtos: A sweet yeast-risen ritual bread offered to the church on major religious holidays and distributed to the people attending the Mass. A relief representation is usually sealed on top to mark this bread offering.

Aloussià: Lye - also known as alissìva in Greek. A mixture of water and ash boiled and drained.

Amigdalotò: Marzipan. A sweet made with almond and sugar (see Recipes).

Anthòtiro: A soft, fatless, unsalted white cheese, made from goat's and sheep's milk. It can be preserved in the fridge and there is also a hard type. The word stems from anthos + tiros (cream + cheese).

Apàkia: Dry-salted pork marinated in vinegar and smoke-dried with aromatic herbs. Rolled in a layer of spices and seasonings acquiring in this way a characteristic sourish and flavourful taste.

Avgokalàmara: Confectionary in the shape of a cone or knot. Deep fried, its basic ingredients consist of flour and honey (see Recipes).

Avgolèmono: Creamy sauce of beaten eggs and lemon juice, poured over several dishes of Cretan cuisine.

Baklavàs: A sweet of oriental origin. It has layers of phyllo pastry and chopped nuts dredged with syrup (see Recipes).

Boubouristì: A specific way of cooking snails (deep-frying), by putting them in hot olive oil with the orifice facing downwards.

Bourekàkia: Small syrup patties, made with phyllo pastry, walnut and almond filling (see Recipes).

Bouréki: A pie with or without phyllo pastry made with mizithra cheese, zucchini, and in some cases potato, as well. It can also be prepared as a dessert with sweet mizithra cheese (see Recipes).

Christòpsomo: Special sweet bread especially made for Christmas, with dough decorations. The name originates etymologically from the Greek words Christòs + psomì (Christ + bread).

Dàkos: Cretan barley or wheat rusk with olive oil, topped with fresh chopped tomato and mizìthra cheese. In Crete, it is also known by the name Koukouvàgia (Owl) (see Recipes).

Dolmadàkia, Dolmàdes: Vine leaves stuffed with rice. The name is of oriental origin (see Recipes).

Fàva: Puree made from broad beans or peas (see Recipes).

Fèta: An internationally famous white, soft or hard cheese originally made from ewe or goat's milk, cut in blocks and matured in brine to give it a sharp acidic and salty taste. It is traditionally kept in wooden barrels and it has a fat and salt content of 35%-45% and 8% respectively. It is usually crumbled or cut into pieces and used in salads.

Gardoùmia: Rolled goat or lamb intestines (stomach, intestines and legs), which can be either cooked in tomato sauce or boiled in avgolèmono sauce.

Gemistà: Stuffed vegetables such as peppers, tomatoes, eggplants or courgettes baked in the oven. The basic ingredient of the stuffing is rice and/or mincemeat (see Recipes).

Giachnerà: Stewed greens, boiled with chopped onion, tomato and olive oil.

Gravièra: Gruyere-like, mature cheese of Cretan origin, with characteristic holes. Made only from sheep's milk (or rarely from mixtures of sheep's and goat's milk), it has a sweetish rich flavour. Its fat and humidity content are 40% and 38% respectively.

Hainìdes: Cretan rebels during the period of Turkish occupation.

Hilopìtes: Very popular homemade noodles. A mixture of flour, eggs, water and salt formed either into long flat ribbons like Fettucini or small squares.

Hilòs: A method for preparing pasta or cereals, in which all the ingredients are boiled, until the cooking liquid is completely absorbed and a sticky and thick mush is obtained. Resembles porridge or frumenty.

Hòntros or Hòndros: Wheat grated through a quern, boiled with milk, and then air dried. It is commonly used to add spice to several dishes. Similar to *trahanàs* (see Recipes).

Kakavià: Fish soup (bouillabaisse), usually made from small fishes. Fishermen's favourite (see Recipes).

Kaltsoùnia / Kalitsoùnia: Small traditional Cretan pastries stuffed with greens and/or cheese. They can be either baked or fried (see Recipes).

Karidotò: Walnut macaroons. A sweet made with ground walnuts dredged with confectioner's sugar (see Recipes).

Kassèri: Slightly salted yellow cheese, with a hard cheddar-like texture made from sheep's or goat's milk. It is usually left to mature at least for three months.

Katimèria from Sèlino: Small fried pies stuffed with cheese, dredged with sugar. The name comes from the area of Sélino, in Hania.

Kefalograviéra: Hard, whitish and fairly salted cheese, made from pasteurised sheep's milk or a mixture of sheep's milk and a very small quantity of goat's milk.

Koftò macaroni: Small, short tubes of pasta. Rigatoni-like, but cut in smaller pieces.

Kokorètsi: Lamb or goat intestines stranded with livers. It is cooked on a spit, over charcoals.

Kourabiès: Baked sugar buns. Flour and cloves constitute the basic ingredients. Dredged with plenty of confectioner's sugar, it is a traditional Christmas sweet (see Recipes).

Krassomezès: Small pieces of meat, cooked in casserole with wine. The name comes from krassì + mezès (wine + appetizer).

Kritharàki pasta: Barley-shaped pasta, similar to rice. Orzo pasta.

Labrokouloùra: Round bread kneaded in several sizes, especially made for Easter. The name comes from labrì + kouloùra (Easter + ring-shaped bread).

Ladorìgani: A mixture of olive oil and oregano, used to baste meat. The name comes from làdi + rìgani (oil + oregano).

Ladotìri: A Greek traditional, salty hard cheese. Made from sheep's milk or mixtures of sheep's milk and goat's milk, it is left to mature and is also preserved in olive oil. The name comes from làdi + tirì (oil + cheese).

Lahanodolmàdes : Cabbage leaves stuffed with rice. The name comes from làhano + *dolmàdes* (cabbage + *dolmàdes*

Lihnaràki or Skaltsoùni: Small traditional Cretan sweets stuffed with cheese. It is the sweet version of *kaltsoùni*, dredged with cinnamon.

Loukoumàdes: Ball-like doughnuts, the size of a tablespoon. Deep-fried in hot oil, they are either dredged with cinnamon, or honey syrup is poured over them (see Recipes).

Magirìtsa: A soup dish, made with small pieces of lamb or goat intestines, cooked with rice and spices or greens. It is considered to be an Easter specialty, enjoyed on Holy Saturday after the Resurrection Mass after midnight.

Malàka or Tiromàlama: A fresh elastic cheese of Cretan origin. Made from goat's milk, it has a high content in fat.

Mangìri or Magìri: Traditional Cretan pasta shaped into squares; made without eggs. When egg is added, then it is shaped into very thin strands of pasta.

Melomakàrona: Small honey oval-shaped cookies soaked in syrup. Made with flour and walnuts. Dredged with cinnamon and sesame seeds, it is a Christmas sweet (see Recipes).

Metòhi: A piece of land, usually the property of a monastery but in a different area, cultivated by the monks or by farmers. Nowadays, the term refers to a piece of farmland as private property.

Mizìthra: A soft, white cream cheese of Cretan origin with a delicate taste because of its minimum content in salt. There is also a sweet type of mizithra cheese.

Moustalevrià: A must-jelly sweet made from fresh grape juice and flour. The name comes from moùstos + alévri (must + flour).

Moustokoùlouro: Cookies with must as their basic ingredient. The name comes from moùstos + kouloùri (must + bread roll).

Neratzoeliès: Olives preserved in bitter orange juice.

Oftò or Optò: Usually referring to roast meat, it is a specific way of cooking in an earthen or traditional oven, on spits or open fire.

Omathiès or Ematiès: Sausages made from swine's large intestine, filled with finely sliced pork meat, *pligoùri* or rice and a small quantity of pork blood.

Oùzo: Traditional anise-flavoured spirit, made from grape marc.

Patoùda: Half moon-shaped pies, filled with walnuts and almonds, dredged with confectioner's sugar (see Recipes).

Petimèzi: Syrupy liquid produced from the condensation of grape must, when boiled over low heat for a fair amount of time.

Pichtì: Generally it refers to the preservation of broth in a solid, transparent form. It is made after boiling the head, legs and leather of swine. After the boning, vinegar, salt, pepper and garlic is added, Pork jelly brawn (see Recipes).

Pilàfi: Rice boiled in meat broth. The broth can come from sheep, goat, or chicken meat. Butter and lemon juice are added after the boiling process is completed (see Recipes).

Pligoùri or Bligoùri: The terms refer to groats and by extension to every dish that may contain groats as a basic ingredient.

Prosforà/Pròsforo/ Litourgìa: Sanctified and consecrated bread dedicated to God. It is etymologically derived from the Greek verb 'prosféro' (offer). It is

Retsìna: used mixed with wine in Greek Orthodox services for the Holy Communion.

White or rose dry wine, flavoured with resin.

Rizàri or Alizàri: Madder (Rubia Tinctorum). A Mediterranean plant with yellowish flowers. The dyeing substance of its root (Alisarin) was used for dyeing since ancient times.

Sarìki: The traditional headdress of Cretan men. Sarikòpita is a traditional pie, which is sarìki shaped.

Sfakianò: Lamb meat cooked in oil, with greens and wine (see Recipes).

Sfougàto: A dish with beaten eggs as the basic ingredient. The eggs are fried and then several other ingredients can be added, such as cheese, greens, sausages, etc. (see Recipes).

Sìglina: Smoke-dried pork, preserved in its own fat.

Skioufihtà: Home made macaroni. The basic ingredients are wheaten flour, water, salt, lemon and a little oil. It is shaped into little curls.

Skordalià: An appetizing dish (garlic paste) made from mashed potato, garlic, fish roe and olive oil (Skòrdo - garlic in Greek). (See Recipes).

Sofagàda/Sofegàda/Sympetheriò: Various fresh vegetables, such as zucchini, eggplants, green beans, etc., cooked together in a casserole.

Soutzoukàkia: Stewed mincemeat - balls in red sauce (see Recipes).

Stàka: Dairy product, which is the fresh cream skimmed off the top of milk (the cream of milk). It is cooked with a little flour and salt and has a very high fat content.

Stakovoùtiro: Butter cream produced from stàka.

Stifàdo: Stew usually made with meat, oil, onions and wine.

Tiganòpites: Fried pies made with plain flour or almond filling.

Tis òras: Grilled food. The phrase is found on the menus of Greek restaurants or tavernas and comes from fagitò + òra (food + hour). Referring to food prepared to order.

Touloupàni/Toulpàni: A piece of white cotton cloth used for the runoff of food. Commonly used for the preparation of dairy products, or sauces e.g. tomato sauce.

Trahanàs: Home made pasta made from air dried wheaten flour and milk, grated through a special metallic sieve, after coming to a boil. It is often served as a soup dish.

Triftoùdia or Triftilidia: A local pasta variety from Crete, shaped like little rice pellets.

Tsakistés (Olives): Cracked green olives preserved in lemon juice. The olives are cracked with a stone.

Tsikoudià/Raki: Traditional Cretan spirit. The distillate of grape marc.

Tsounatòlado: Olive oil produced from a specific variety of olive trees, 'tsounàti'.

Tzatzìki: A cold appetizing dish made with yoghurt, chopped cucumber and garlic.

Xerotìgana: A Cretan traditional confectionary. They are deep fried pastry curls made of dough, dipped in honey syrup. Dredged with sesame seeds (see Recipes).

Xinòhondros: Crushed wheat boiled in sour milk. It can be consumed either fresh or air-dried (see Recipes).

Xobliàstres: Expert craftswomen in villages, usually elderly, talented and experienced in bread decoration.

RECIPES INDEX

BIBLIOGRAPHY

We could not possibly fail to mention our sources, which constitute a source of information and inspiration for the writing of the present book. *"Cretan Healthy Diet - Truths and Secrets"* draws on previous publications by the Prefecture of Hania as well as a series of other books dealing with Cretan diet:

• Prefecture of Hania, *Cretan Diet*, Hania 1998

• Prefecture of Hania, *Proceedings of Agricultural August 1999*, Hania 1999

• Prefecture of Hania, *Proceedings of Agricultural August 2000*, Hania 2000

• Prefecture of Hania, *Proceedings of Agricultural August 2001*, Hania 2001

• Prefecture of Hania, *The Olive Tree, Olive Oil, Health & Culture*, Hania 2002

• Mirsini Lambraki, *Oil, Tastes and Culture of 5.000 yeas*, Ellinika Grammata, Athens, 1999

• Nikos & Maria Psilakis - Ilias Kastanas, *The Culture of the Olive Tree, Olive Oil*, Karmanor, Heraklion 1999

• Nikos & Maria Psilakis, Traditional Cretan Cuisine, Karmanor, Heraklion 1995

THE BOOK
CRETAN HEALTHY DIET – TRUTHS AND SECRETS
WAS PUBLISHED BY KERKYRA PUBLICATIONS,
PRINTED AND BOUND BY MULTIMEDIA S.A.
IN 1,500 COPIES
ATHENS, AUGUST 2005